Resources and Environment

Michael Raw

UNWIN HYMAN

FOR EDWARD AND OLIVER

Published by
UNWIN HYMAN LIMITED
15–17 Broadwick Street
London W1V 1FP

© Michael Raw 1989

**British Library Cataloguing in Publication
Data**

Raw, Michael
   Resources and environment.—
   (Understanding applied geography).
   1. Natural resources – For schools
   I. Title
   333.7

ISBN 0–7135–2845–1

Printed in Great Britain by
the Alden Press, Osney Mead, Oxford

Resources and Environment

Contents

(*Colour section appears between pages 144 and 145*)

Acknowledgements

The author and publisher would like to thank the following for permission to use photographs:

Aberdeen Journals 2.59
Aerofilms 1.5
Aerophoto Schiphol 2.2
J. Allan Cash Limited 1.6a, 1.6b, 1.29, 1.46c, 1.48, 2.19, 2.51, 2.88, 3.19, 3.30b, 3.30c.
Amax Coal Company 2.7
Associated Press 1.49b, 2.44
Martin Bond 2.78
British Coal, Yorkshire Regional Photographic Department 2.18, 2.20
Cambridge University Air Photographs 1.16, 3.13a
Camera Press 2.94a (photo by Leonard Burt), 2.94b (photo by Reto Hugin)
Central Electricity Generating Board 2.16
Colorific 1.54a (© Jim Howard, 1982), 1.54c (© Martin Rogers, 1985)
Durham County Council Planning Department 2.21a and b
The Financial Times 2.39
Stan Gamester, Tyne and Wear 1.56
Geoscience Features Picture Library 2.47
Paul Glendell 3.39, 2.27, 3.9a
The Guardian 2.34
Horizon Holidays 3.42
David Keith Jones 3.56 a–e
Landform Slides 3.25
Nordisk Pressefoto 2.76, 2.85
Northumbrian Water Authority 1.15
Jane Olivier Publicity (photos by Willie Alleyne Associates) 3.35a and b
Oxfam 2.3
Panos Pictures 2.91 (© Geoff Barnard)
Photo Source 1.21a, 1.54b (© Peter L. Gould, 1974), 2.55, 2.57, 2.62
Picture House Limited, Bradford 3.9b
Popperfoto 1.46a, 2.73, 3.26, 3.30a, 3.30d
Press Association 2.32
Scottish Tourist Board 2.50
Shell 2.49

Sri Lankan High Commission 1.34
Philip Steele/ICCE 1.46b, 2.28
Svenskt Pressfoto 1.30
Swedish Embassy 2.31 (© André Maslennikov/IBL)
Swiss National Tourist Office 3.48b, c and d
Thames Water 1.21b, 1.59
United Kingdom Atomic Energy Authority 2.65, 2.77
West Air Photography 3.33
Derek G. Widdicombe, Countrywide Photographic Library 1.38a, 3.17b, c and d

We would also like to acknowledge that some of the illustrations are adapted or redrawn from other published works:

Figure 2.16 *Leeds and its Environment*, by Dickinson and Atkinson, *TIBG* 1985, reproduced by permission of Basil Blackwell
Figure 1.31a & b *Sri Lanka: Land People and Economy*, B.L. Johnson and M. Scrivenor, Heinemann Education, 1981
Figure 1.52 'Water Resource Management Issues on the Great Lakes: some issues in the 1980's', D. Kay and A. McDonald, University of Leeds Regional Canadian Studies Centre, 1985
Figure 2.84 & 2.85 *Atlas of Renewable Energy Resources: In the United Kingdom and North America*, L.R. Mustoe, Wiley, 1984
Figure 4.22 *The Changing Geography of the United Kingdom*, Ed. R.J. Johnston and J.C. Doornkamp, Metheun and Co., 1983

The simulation exercise on page 33 also appears in *Teaching Geography*, January 1989.

The publishers have made every effort to trace copyright holders, but if they have inadvertently overlooked any they will be pleased to make the necessary arrangements.

Preface

Understanding Applied Geography: Resources and Environment is a complementary text to *Understanding Human Geography*, written for GCSE courses in geography and environmental studies. Its style and approach are similar to the earlier text, and its focus – environmental resources – is a key area in most syllabuses.

The book fulfils the objectives of the National Criteria. Detailed case studies from DCs (with special emphasis given to the UK) and LDCs underline the contrasts in resource use and development at global, national and local scales. Structured exercises, designed to develop understanding and skills, are an integral part of the book: they are based on a wide range of stimulus material, including OS maps, graphs, diagrams, photos, and newspaper cuttings, and statistical tables. They invite active involvement by pupils, which I believe helps to generate enthusiasm and sustain interest. I also hope that teachers will use the exercises selectively, and will find them helpful when organising classwork and homework for their pupils.

Throughout the book I have tried to give prominence to those environmental issues which have a geographical dimension. Increasingly, issues such as acid rain, radwaste disposal, and coastal pollution are everyday news items, of which our pupils already have some awareness. As teachers and geographers it is our task to give pupils a basic understanding of these issues, and, more importantly, a general framework through which they can evaluate them and then arrive at their own opinions and judgements. Although I have tried to present these issues objectively, you will know that the teaching of values and attitudes is a notoriously difficult area. May I therefore apologise in advance if my training as a geographer has resulted in any (unintended) environmental bias!

M.D.R
Bradford 1988

Part One

Water resources

No resource is more vital than water. Industry in particular has a huge appetite for water: for example, it takes 450 000 litres of water to make a single motor car, and 200 000 litres to produce one tonne of steel. Agriculture is only possible when sufficient water is available either directly from rainfall, or from rivers and wells. At home we each use an average of 150 litres of water a day on activities such as washing, bathing, cooking, flushing the toilet and so on (Fig. 1.1b). Most of these ways of using water make it dirty, and, as a result, streams, rivers, lakes and the sea become polluted. As we shall see later, this pollution increasingly conflicts with the growing demand for water for recreation and leisure, and for a clean environment.

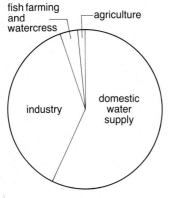

Figure 1.1a Water abstractions by purposes in England and Wales

Figure 1.1b Average household water use (130 litres per person per day)

Water supply and the water cycle

The oceans and seas cover seven-tenths of the earth's surface and act as gigantic stores or *reservoirs* for the world's water resources (Fig. 1.2). Indeed the earth is so dominated by water that on first viewing it from space, astronauts christened it the 'blue planet'. Yet, in spite of its abundance, only a small fraction of the

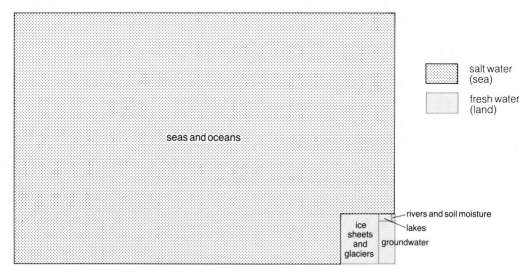

Figure 1.2 Distribution of the world's water resources

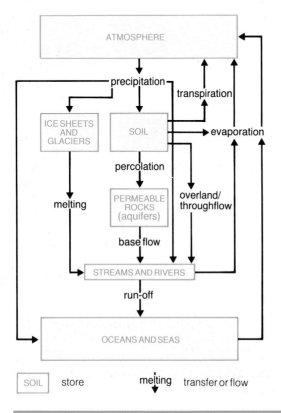

Figure 1.3 The water cycle

world's water is useful as a resource: 97% is salt water, unsuitable for drinking, agriculture and most other purposes; and of the 3% which is fresh water, three-quarters is locked up in the ice caps of Antarctica and Greenland. So we are left with less than 1% of the world's total water resources, in streams, rivers, lakes, soil and permeable rocks, which can be directly used by people. Fortunately, water is a *renewable* resource which is constantly recycled between the oceans, the atmosphere, and the land surface (Fig. 1.3). People use water resources by intervening at various stages in this *water cycle* (Fig. 1.4). Most intervention occurs at the *run-off* stage by the regulation of river flow and the removal of water from rivers. Large amounts of *groundwater* are also obtained, from wells sunk into water-bearing rocks or *aquifers*. However, so far there has not been much intervention at the rainfall stage, apart from 'seeding' rain clouds with chemicals in order to increase rainfall amounts.

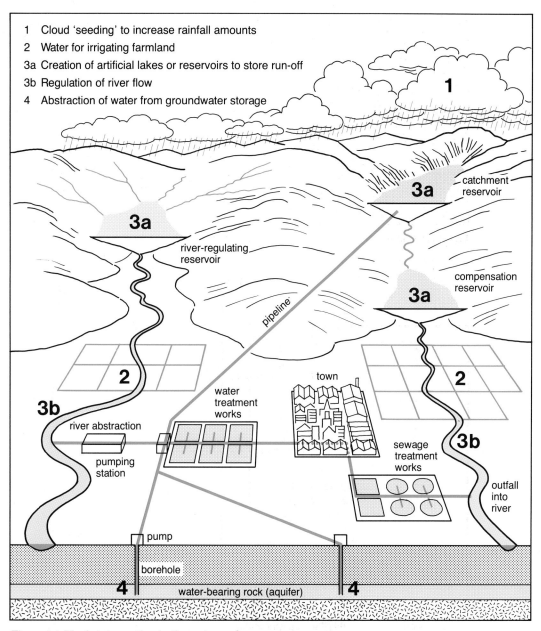

1   Cloud 'seeding' to increase rainfall amounts
2   Water for irrigating farmland
3a Creation of artificial lakes or reservoirs to store run-off
3b Regulation of river flow
4   Abstraction of water from groundwater storage

Figure 1.4 Man's intervention in the water cycle

Exercise

Identify the missing words in the paragraphs below and copy the paragraphs into your exercise book under the heading 'Water Cycle'.

The water _____ consists of several _____ where water is stored, and a number of _____ which transfer the water between them. The largest reservoir is the _____ water of the oceans and seas. By comparison, fresh water reservoirs are small, and the bulk of fresh water resources are frozen in the _____ of Antarctica and Greenland. Fresh water is also stored briefly in rivers, lakes and the soil, and as _____ in permeable rocks.

The two most important flows in the water cycle are the transfer of water from the earth's surface to the atmosphere by _____, and the return of this water to the earth's surface by _____. Most precipitation is either rain or _____ and 86% falls directly into the oceans and seas. The remainder, which falls on the land, eventually finds its way into streams and rivers and flows into the ocean basins and seas.

precipitation, groundwater, cycle, snow, salt, reservoirs, evaporation, ice caps, flows.

Water supply in the UK

The UK, situated on the western margins of Europe, lies in the belt of prevailing westerly winds. These moisture-laden winds blow uninterrupted across 5000 kilometres of ocean, and bring abundant, year-round precipitation to the UK. Few areas of the world have a climate which is so strongly influenced by the ocean.

The average precipitation in England and Wales in a year is 912 millimetres. However, this figure conceals wide variations: on exposed western hills in Wales and the Lake District (Fig. 1.5), precipitation can reach 2500 millimetres a year, whereas in the lowlands of eastern England, 600–700 millimetres a year is typical

Figure 1.5 The Forest of Bowland forms a moorland plateau, between 400 and 500 metres high, in North West England. It receives up to 2000 mm of precipitation a year, and is an important catchment area for water supplied to towns in central Lancashire.

(Fig. 1.7c). Whatever the amount, precipitation in all regions is fairly evenly spread throughout the year, and droughts such as those of summer 1976 (Fig. 1.6b) and spring 1981 are rare exceptions. Indeed the British holiday-maker and cricket fan are only too aware that rain has to be expected in a typical British summer.

Figure 1.6a The Berkshire Downs. This chalk upland is porous, with water stored underground in the chalk aquifer. It is protected as an area of outstanding natural beauty

Figure 1.6b The dried-up bed of the River Derwent at Seathwaite, Cumbria, during the drought of 1976. Normally Seathwaite is one of the wettest places in England

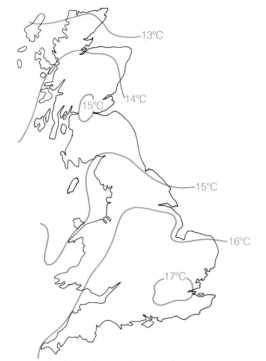

Figure 1.7a Mean July temperatures in Britain

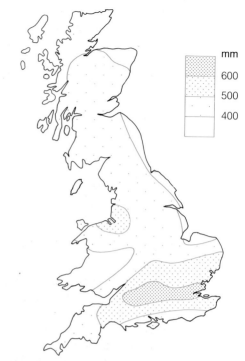

Figure 1.7b Mean annual evaporation in Britain

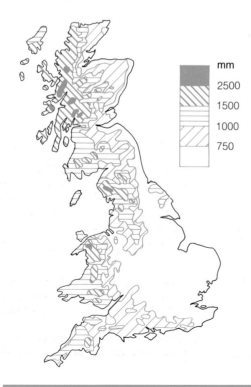

Exercise

Figure 1.8b is a relief section between South Wales and East Anglia drawn along a line from Swansea to Ipswich.

1 Trace this section into your exercise book, and then using Figure 1.8a draw a similar section to show changes in average yearly precipitation between Swansea and Ipswich. Use a vertical scale of 1 centimetre to 1000 millimetres for your graph.

2 Name the areas of highest and lowest precipitation and describe the effect of relief on precipitation along the section.

3 Give *two* reasons for changes in precipitation along the section.

Figure 1.7c Mean annual precipitation in Britain

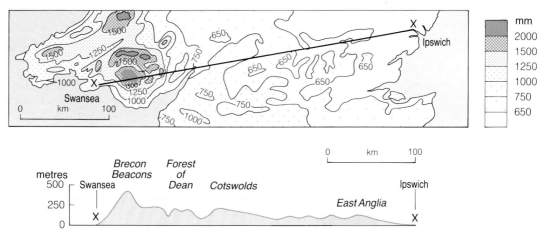

Figure 1.8a *(top)* Mean annual precipitation in southern Britain. 1.8b *(below)* Relief section from South Wales to East Anglia

Water supply in England and Wales is the responsibility of ten regional *water authorities* (Fig. 1.9) whose boundaries follow the *watersheds* of large *river basins* such as the Severn, Trent and Thames. The water resources available to each authority are largely controlled by amounts of precipitation. For instance, areas such as Wales and the South West which receive a high average precipitation (Fig. 1.7c) have plentiful supplies. But in areas of low precipitation like Thames and Southern, there is only just sufficient water to meet demand. Apart from precipitation, water resources also depend on levels of *evaporation* (Fig. 1.7b). Areas of high precipitation are often cloudy and cool, which reduces evaporation and increases the amount of water that is available. In the warmer and sunnier lowlands it is just the opposite: here higher rates of evaporation increase water loss, and reduce further the already limited water supplies caused by low precipitation. Thus, when we measure the water resources of an area we must look at the *difference* between precipitation and evaporation – the *residual precipitation*.

Figure 1.9 Water authority regions in England and Wales

Exercise

Study the two graphs in Figure 1.10 which show precipitation and evaporation at Shrewsbury and Buxton. Shrewsbury, which is 91 metres above sea level, has a climate typical of lowland England. Buxton, at 305 metres above sea level, represents upland areas in England.

1 How much more precipitation does Buxton receive than Shrewsbury? Give your answer in both millimetres and as a percentage.

2 Refer to Figures 1.7 and 1.11 and suggest *two* reasons for the low precipitation at Shrewsbury.

3 Explain why evaporation is higher at Shrewsbury.

4 Calculate the residual precipitation at Shrewsbury and Buxton. How much greater is residual precipitation at Buxton than Shrewsbury: a) in millimetres, b) as a percentage?

5 Taking account of your calculations in the previous section what would you say is the more important factor responsible for differences in water resources between Shrewsbury and Buxton – precipitation or evaporation? Explain your answer.

Exercise

Look carefully at Fig. 1.11 and complete the following:

1 What name is given to slopes that a) face *towards* the prevailing wind and b) face *away* from the prevailing wind.

2 Give two reasons why leeward slopes are drier than windward slopes.

3 Give two reasons why water resources are smaller in the east, than in the west.

4 Explain why it is so wet in the western mountains.

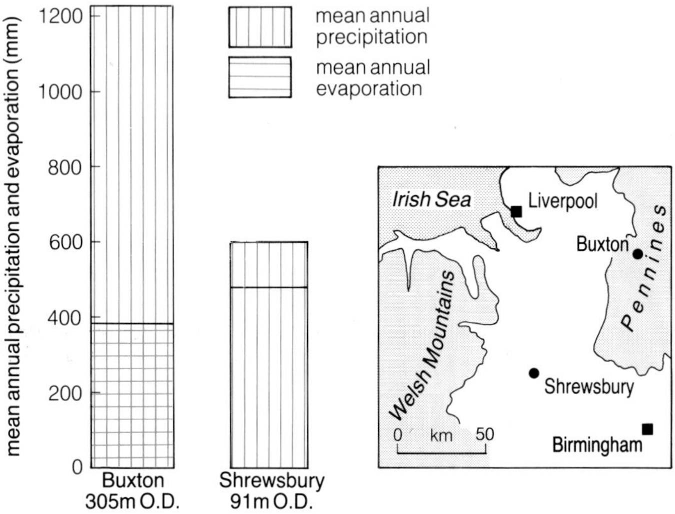

Figure 1.10 Precipitation and evaporation in highland and lowland Britain

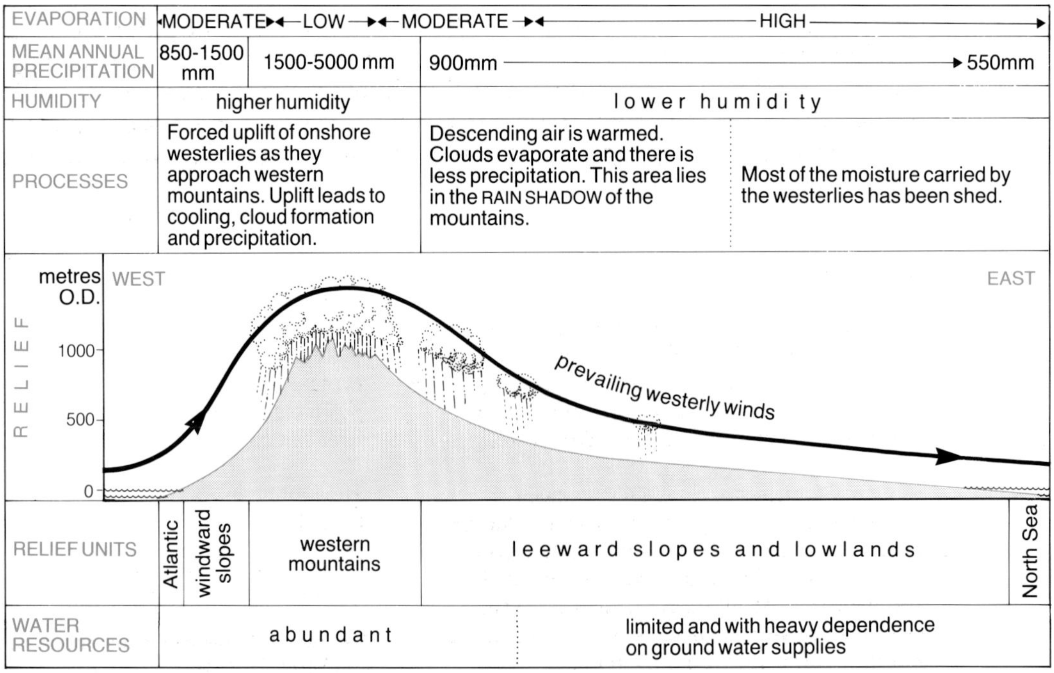

Figure 1.11 Precipitation and water resources in the UK

EVAPORATION	MODERATE	LOW	MODERATE	HIGH
MEAN ANNUAL PRECIPITATION	850-1500 mm	1500-5000 mm	900mm → 550mm	
HUMIDITY	higher humidity		lower humidity	
PROCESSES	Forced uplift of onshore westerlies as they approach western mountains. Uplift leads to cooling, cloud formation and precipitation.		Descending air is warmed. Clouds evaporate and there is less precipitation. This area lies in the RAIN SHADOW of the mountains.	Most of the moisture carried by the westerlies has been shed.

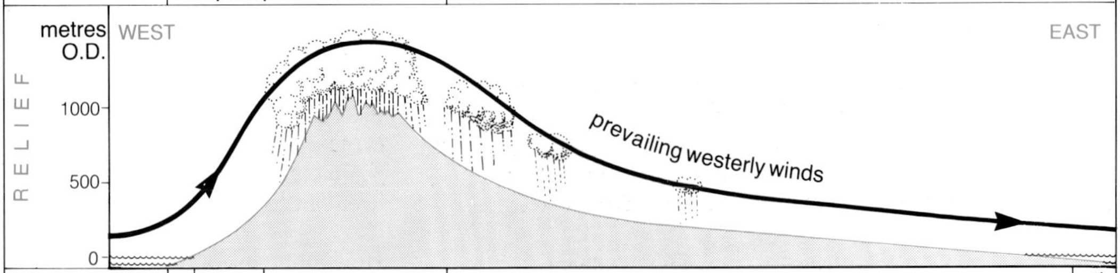

RELIEF UNITS	Atlantic	windward slopes	western mountains	leeward slopes and lowlands	North Sea
WATER RESOURCES	abundant			limited and with heavy dependence on ground water supplies	

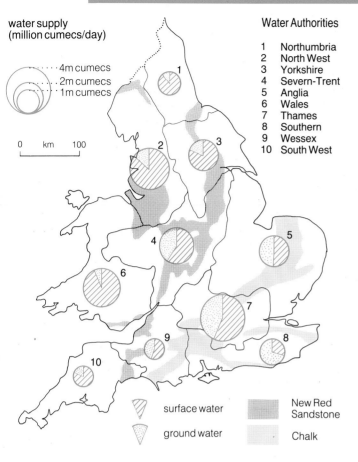

water supply
(million cumecs/day)

.... 4m cumecs
... 2m cumecs
.. 1m cumecs

0   km   100

Water Authorities

1   Northumbria
2   North West
3   Yorkshire
4   Severn-Trent
5   Anglia
6   Wales
7   Thames
8   Southern
9   Wessex
10 South West

surface water

ground water

New Red Sandstone

Chalk

Figure 1.12 Water supply for domestic, industrial and agricultural use in England and Wales

The water authorities differ in the extent to which they rely on surface water and groundwater. Areas which depend most on surface water from rivers and lakes, are in the north and west (Figs 1.12 and 1.5). Here the rocks are mainly impermeable, and most precipitation quickly finds its way into streams and rivers. In contrast, in the south and east, *permeable* rocks such as chalk and sandstone are widespread (Fig. 1.6a). A large proportion of precipitation sinks into these aquifers where it is stored and released slowly into streams and rivers.

Water demand in the UK

The demand for water in the UK is rising steadily. Currently the water authorities in England and Wales supply around 16 million cubic metres (cumecs) a day (Fig. 1.13). By the year 2011 it is estimated that this figure will have risen to 20 million cumecs. Although there is sufficient water to meet this demand there is a major problem of geography: quite simply precipitation does not fall in sufficient amounts in the areas where it is most needed.

Exercise

1 Using Table 1.1 on page 18, compare in a sentence or two the *total* water resources available in England and Wales with
   a) current demand of 16 million cumecs/day,
   b) future demand of 20 million cumecs/day.

2 Plot the information in Table 1.1 as a scattergraph like Figure 1.14. Notice that in Figure 1.14 values for the first three water authorities in the table have been plotted for you, and that population totals and water resources have been divided into three broad groups – large, medium and small.

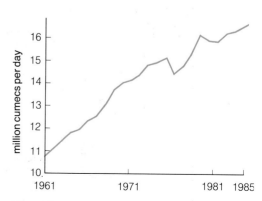

Figure 1.13 Growth of water supply in England and Wales 1961–85

3 When you have completed your scattergraph, compile a table (like the one below), and group the water authorities into three categories. For example, the scattergraph shows that in the North West water resources are large, while population (or demand) is medium. We assume that in this region water supply is likely to exceed demand. In the Anglia region water resources are small and demand is medium-sized. Here, demand is likely to exceed supply, with possible water shortages in future.

	Water supply	
Water supply exceeds demand	and demand are matched	Water demand exceeds supply
North West	Northumbria	Anglia

4 Study your completed table and the map of water authority regions (Fig. 1.9). In which parts of the country does a) water supply generally exceed demand, b) demand generally exceed water supply? Describe the overall pattern in a few sentences.

5 Which authority has a) the most favourable, b) the least favourable balance between supply and demand? Refer to Figures 1.7a,b,c and Table 1.1 and explain the differences in water resources between these two authorities.

6 In 1985 the South West received over 12 million tourists. Suggest some problems which this influx might create for water supplies in the region.

Table 1.1 Supply and demand for water in England and Wales

	Population (millions)	Water resources (million cumecs/day)
Anglia	5.073	4.10
North West	6.885	10.83
Northumbria	2.642	4.17
Severn-Trent	8.247	6.48
South West	1.422	7.40
Southern	3.900	3.24
Thames	11.539	2.95
Wales	3.308	18.64
Wessex	2.346	4.07
Yorkshire	4.558	5.13

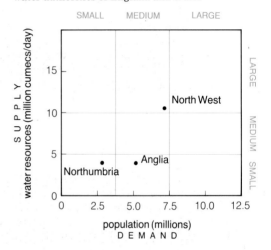

Figure 1.14 Water resources: supply and demand in water authorities of England and Wales

The ten water authorities have the task of meeting the rising demand for water in England and Wales in future. At the moment any large scale *water transfer schemes* between authorities are unlikely owing to the high costs involved. Consequently, water authorities will be forced to consider ways of developing additional resources from *within* their own areas. The next section describes the different approaches of the Northumbria and Thames water authorities towards this problem.

Kielder Water: western Europe's largest man-made lake

In Northumberland, close to the Scottish border, the North Tyne River has been dammed to create Kielder Water, western Europe's largest artificial lake (Fig. 1.15). Kielder Water, which regulates the flow of the North Tyne, allows water to be transferred by a regional water grid to the whole of North East England. Kielder was planned in the early 1970s when demand for water in the North East was expected to rise rapidly. As in the UK generally, there was no overall shortage of water in the region; the problem was that water supplies were in the wrong place! The wettest areas – the North Pennines – receive over 1200 millimetres of precipitation a year, but these areas are largely uninhabited. However, the driest areas, which are near the coast and barely average 700 millimetres a year, include the conurbations of Tyneside and Teesside, and contain the bulk of the region's population and heavy industry (Fig. 1.16).

Figure 1.15 Kielder Water, formed by the damming of the North Tyne Valley, has not only greatly increased water resources in North East England, but has developed into one of the region's principal tourist attractions

Figure 1.16 Steel, chemical and oil-refining industries at the mouth of the River Tees in North East England. The Kielder project will ensure a plentiful supply of water to these industries until well into the twenty-first century

Kielder, completed in 1984, has effectively doubled the North East's water resources, guaranteeing supplies until well into the next century. Water from Kielder is distributed via the region's three major rivers: the Tyne, Wear and Tees. First, the water travels 58 kilometres down the North Tyne and Tyne to Riding Mill (Fig. 1.17) where it is taken out and transferred along 32 kilometres of tunnels to top-up the flows of the Wear and Tees. The water is finally taken out of these rivers near to the coast, and close to the main centres of demand. After treatment which improves the quality of the water to make it drinkable, it is distributed through the mains to households and industrial users.

Exercise

1 Study Figure 1.17 and explain why the River Tyne is likely to have larger water resources than either the River Wear or River Tees.

2 Suggest possible advantages of transferring water to users by means of rivers rather than by pipelines or aqueducts. Can you think of any disadvantages?

3 How do you think that the Kielder scheme will assist flood control on the River Tyne?

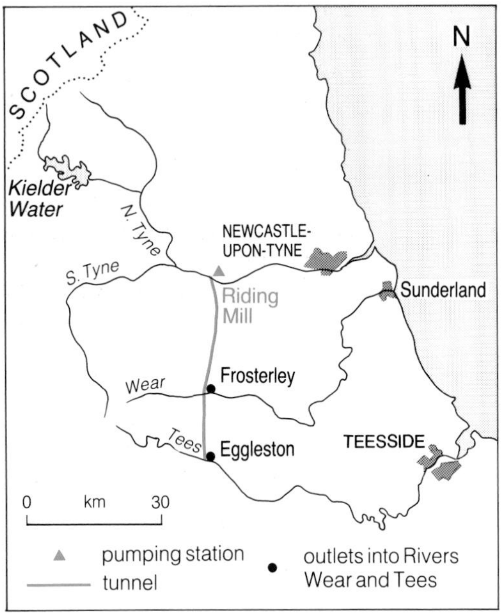

Figure 1.17 *(right)* Kielder regional water transfer scheme

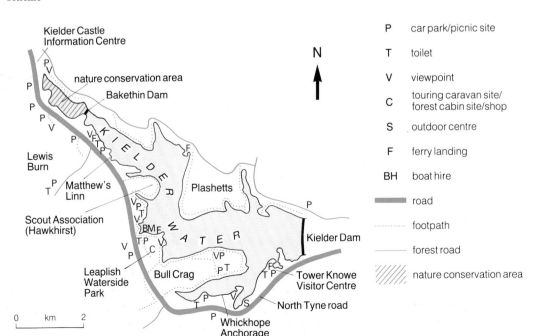

Figure 1.18 The Kielder project and recreation

Kielder is more than just a water supply scheme. It includes a small hydroelectric power (HEP) station which provides electricity for the villages and hamlets of the North Tyne valley. More importantly, it is fast developing into the largest water-based leisure complex in the UK. The main recreational attractions, which are connected by a new road along the south side of the lake (Fig. 1.18), include a visitor centre, picnic sites, mooring areas for motor boats and cruisers, caravanning sites and facilities for angling. In contrast, the lake's northern shore is being left as a wild area, covered by forest, and only accessible on foot, horseback and by boat.

Exercise

The following leisure activities are available at Kielder:

walking   canoeing   sub-aqua
fishing   rowing   swimming
sailing   wind-surfing   motor boating
camping   water-skiing   bird watching

1 Find out which activities are likely to conflict with each other by constructing a matrix similar to Figure 1.19. Where there is little likelihood of conflict (for example between walking and fishing) insert '0' in the appropriate box. Where the possibility of conflict is high (for example between water-skiing and swimming) insert 'X'.

2 Count up the number of 'X's for each activity and list the five activities which cause most conflict.

3 Suggest ways in which recreational activities at Kielder could be managed to reduce conflict.

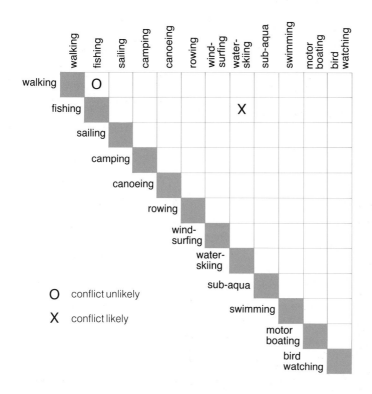

Figure 1.19 Leisure activities and conflict at Kielder Water

O   conflict unlikely

X   conflict likely

London: managing the capital's water supply

Thames has the smallest water resources of any water authority and yet it must supply the largest number of people – almost 11.5 million consumers. Nearly half of all Thames water consumers live in London, which in addition to its own population receives 21.5 million tourists a year. Clearly in order to meet this huge demand the region's water resources must be very carefully managed.

London's water supply comes from two sources: the River Thames, and the chalk aquifer beneath the capital. Today the River Thames provides Londoners with 70% of their water. This water is taken out of the river between Windsor and Teddington (Fig. 1.20); below Teddington the Thames is tidal and even with modern treatment methods its water is unfit for drinking. After the water has been taken from the river it is stored in several large reservoirs on the Thames' *flood plain* (Figs 1.20 and 1.21b), before treatment and distribution through the mains.

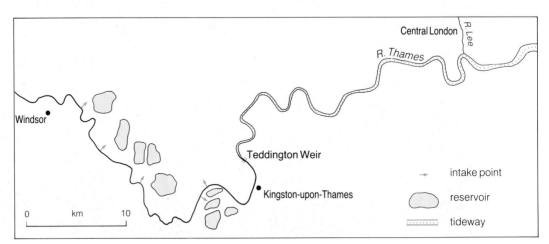

Figure 1.20 London's water supply from the River Thames

Figure 1.21a The River Thames near Marlow, upstream of Teddington Lock

London lies at the centre of a saucer-shaped rock structure known as the London Basin (Fig. 1.22) which is the source of its groundwater supplies. The highest points of the Basin are around the rim where chalk outcrops to form the Chiltern Hills and North Downs. Rain and snow falling on these hills quickly seeps into the porous chalk and flows by gravity through the cracks and pores in the rock towards the centre of the Basin. In the central area the chalk is covered by thick layers of clay and sand.

The first borehole was sunk into the chalk aquifer in London in 1823. Thereafter, development was rapid, with several thousand boreholes drilled between 1850 and 1939. However, little thought was given to the management of supplies, and as the rate of water removal exceeded the rate of recharge by rainfall, the *water table* fell

Figure 1.21b Water storage reservoirs on the Thames flood plain at Hampton

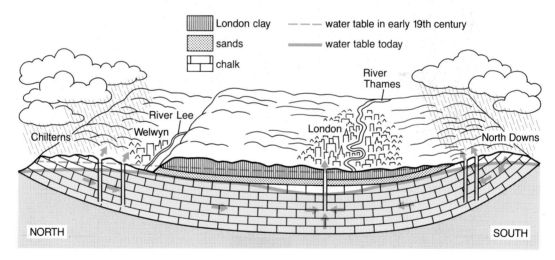

Figure 1.22 The London Basin: underground water resources

and yields declined. Thus in the post-war period London was forced to turn to the River Thames (and its tributary the River Lee) for the bulk of its water supplies. Improvements in methods of treating river water, and the much lower levels of pollution in the Thames in recent years, helped to make this possible. Meanwhile, as the use of groundwater has decreased, the water table under London has started to rise, although it will be another 40 years before it returns to its natural level.

In the last 20 years water supply in the London area has only just managed to keep ahead of demand. Figure 1.23 suggests that unless additional resources are developed, the capital could face a shortage of water by the 1990s. In order to tackle this problem, the water authority is undertaking two schemes. First it plans to take an extra 200 000 cumecs/day from the River Thames, which will be

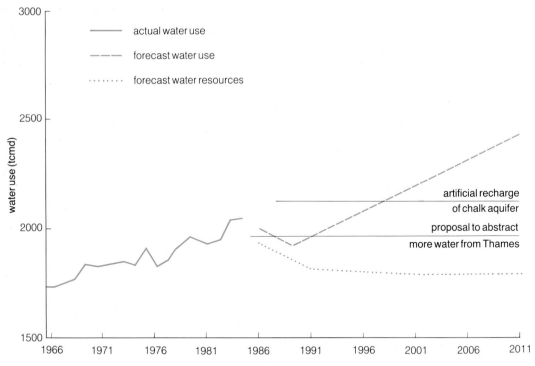

Figure 1.23 Water supply in London 1986–2011 (in thousand cubic metres/day – tcmd)

sufficient to meet demand for five years; and second, it plans to recharge the chalk artificially using the surplus water available in winter from the mains. Water will be injected into the chalk aquifer through boreholes, where it will be stored until needed during dry summers.

Exercise

We have seen that there are two sources of water supply: surface water and groundwater. What are the advantages of groundwater over surface water supplies? Write a paragraph, which covers the following points of comparison: water losses (ie evaporation), water quality (pollution), cost (eg building reservoirs compared to underground storage), effect on the environment (eg reservoirs).

In the long term neither increased removal of water from the Thames nor artificial recharge schemes, will solve London's water supply problems. Several long-term solutions (all of them very costly) have been proposed including the enlargement of existing reservoirs, and the re-use of sewage, which at present is discharged into the Tideway. More ambitious are proposals to build a regulating reservoir (like Kielder) in the headwaters of the Thames and use the Thames flood barrier at Woolwich as a dam to 'pond' water in London, thus turning the river into a fresh water lake! However, both schemes would face enormous practical difficulties, and a more likely option is to import water from other regions. The idea of transferring water from the River Severn to top-up flows in the Thames has been closely studied (Fig. 1.24), and although very expensive, this scheme could be the long-term solution to London's water supply problems.

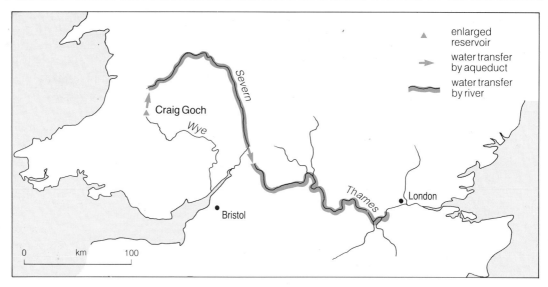

Figure 1.24 Proposed Severn-Thames water transfer

Hydroelectric power: the example of Norway and Sweden

Hydroelectric power (HEP) produced by the force of running water driving a generator, is an *inexhaustible* source of energy. This gives HEP an advantage over fossil fuels like coal and oil, which are non-renewable. Furthermore, unlike fossil fuels and nuclear energy, HEP is *pollution-free*. However, the development of HEP can sometimes damage the environment: valleys may be flooded to create storage reservoirs, and power station buildings and overhead power lines can be an intrusion in the landscape.

Norway and Sweden are Europe's two largest producers of HEP, and both rely heavily on this source of energy. In Norway 77% of the country's energy consumption and all of its electricity, is supplied by HEP. Sweden is less dependent, but even there, 25% of the total energy and 56% of the electricity comes from HEP (Fig. 1.25). Conditions for HEP production are especially

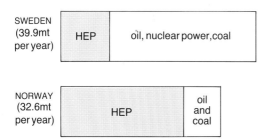

Figure 1.25 Energy consumption in Norway and Sweden (in million tonnes of oil equivalent)

favourable in Norway. The high mountain plateaux or *fjell* of southern Norway have abundant rainfall which is both reliable and evenly spread throughout the year (Figs 1.26 and 1.27). The *fjell* are glaciated uplands, with many lakes acting as natural reservoirs and regulating the flow of the rivers. Although most rivers in southern Norway are quite short, glaciers in the past gouged-out huge *glacial troughs* giving vertical differences in height between the plateaux and valley floors of up to 2000 metres. Such height differences create high *heads* of water, and give massive potential for HEP.

It is fortunate for Norway that the main area of HEP production is also the area of greatest demand for electricity (Figs 1.28 and 1.31): Norway's four largest cities – Oslo, Bergen, Trondheim and Stavanger – are all situated in the southern part of the country. Norway still has large untapped resources of HEP, particularly in the west and in Nordland county (Fig 1.28). However, little remains to be developed in the more densely populated areas around the capital, Oslo. Figure 1.28 shows that not all of the remaining resources will be developed. Resistance by conservationists to the flooding of valleys for new HEP projects has led to several areas of high potential being protected.

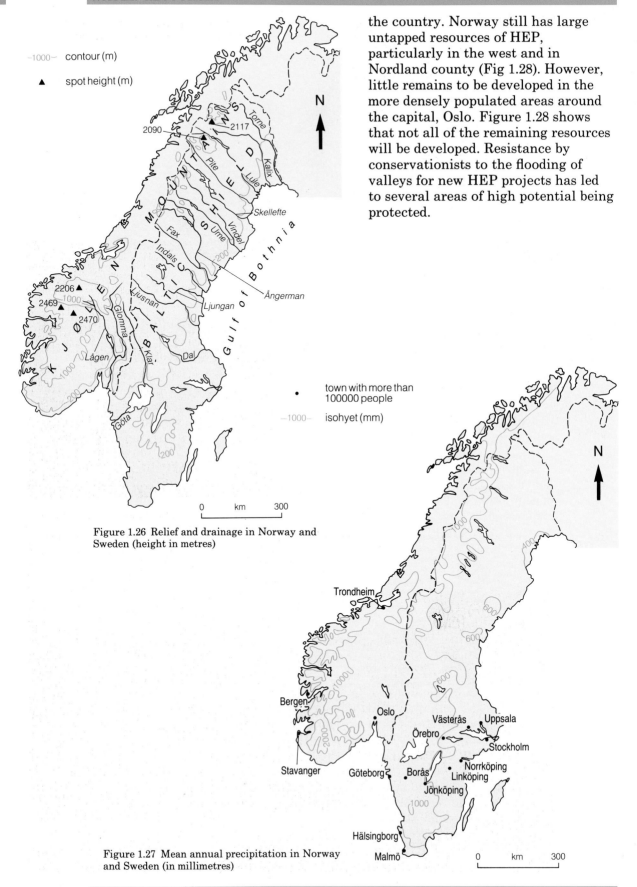

Figure 1.26 Relief and drainage in Norway and Sweden (height in metres)

Figure 1.27 Mean annual precipitation in Norway and Sweden (in millimetres)

HEP resources

protected

developed

remaining

Figure 1.28 HEP resources in Norway: HEP potential and the degree of HEP development in each county

Figure 1.29 HEP station at Rjukan, southern Norway. Glacial valleys, cut deep into the fjell plateaux provide high 'heads' of water, ideal for HEP generation

Figure 1.30 A large HEP station on the Lule River in northern Sweden

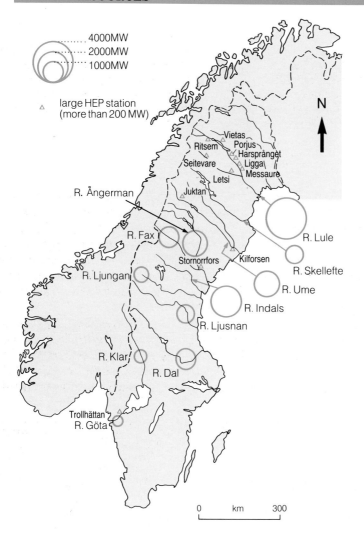

Figure 1.31 HEP production of rivers in Sweden

HEP is Sweden's only major domestic source of energy. There are nearly one thousand HEP stations scattered throughout the country. Most are very small, but in the far north there are several large stations, such as Porjus and Harsprånget on the Lule River (Figs 1.31). Conditions for HEP are not as good as in Norway. The north is the best area, but even here low and often unreliable precipitation, and a prolonged winter freeze cause problems. However, the rivers of the region are long and powerful, flowing from the Kjölen mountains close to the Norwegian border, across the Baltic Shield, to the Gulf of Bothnia (Fig. 1.31). Long glacial lakes interrupt their courses, and provide ideal natural reservoirs, which regulate river flow. The main rivers for HEP are the Lule, Ume, Ångerman and Indals (Fig. 1.31). In southern Sweden, only the Göta River has significant HEP potential.

While most of Sweden's HEP is generated in the north, the main centres of population and demand are in the south. As a result, electricity has to be transmitted over distances of more than 1000 kilometres. In order to reduce energy losses a high voltage grid has been in use for many years. Sweden's remaining untapped HEP reserves are concentrated in the far north close to the Arctic Circle. At the moment it seems unlikely that these reserves will be developed; the Swedish parliament has decreed that the four remaining, free-flowing rivers of the north – the Torne, Kalix, Pite and Vindel – should be protected for environmental reasons.

Exercise

Read through this section on HEP in Norway and Sweden and study Figures 1.28–131. Summarise the main features of HEP production in Norway and Sweden in a table in your exercise book, and try to bring out the main differences between them. Use the following headings in your table: dependence on HEP, physical conditions for HEP, location of main producing areas, location of main consuming areas, future potential, problems, conservationist policies.

The Mahaweli Development Scheme, Sri Lanka

Sri Lanka is a small island of nearly 16 million people, situated just off the southern tip of India. With a Gross Domestic Product (GDP) of only £190 per person per year, Sri Lanka is by any standards poor. In the past, agriculture has suffered through lack of irrigation, making the country heavily dependent on imported foodstuffs, especially rice. Industrial development has been hampered by a shortage of energy, and high levels of unemployment have been a serious problem for many years. To make matters worse, the population is growing rapidly, and will exceed 20 million by the end of the century.

Against this dismal background the Sri Lankan government in 1977 decided to speed up the Mahaweli Development Scheme, which was originally planned to cover the period from 1970 to 2000. This *multi-purpose* project covers 39% of the whole island, and aims to develop fully the water and energy resources of the Mahaweli Ganga, the country's largest river, and the agricultural potential of the

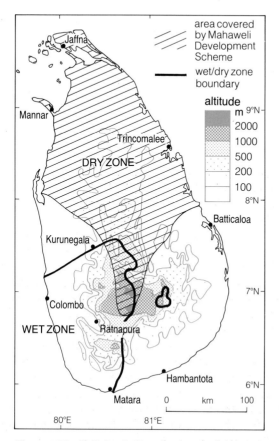

Figure 1.32a Relief and climatic zones in Sri Lanka. (After Johnson and Scrivener)

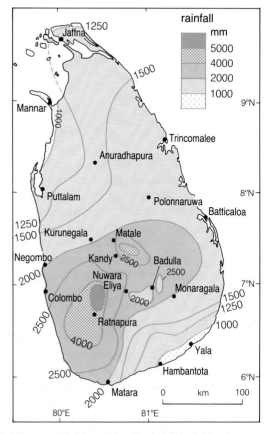

Figure 1.32b Mean annual rainfall in Sri Lanka. (After Johnson and Scrivener)

Dry Zone (Fig. 1.32a). As a result of the scheme, surplus water from the Mahaweli, which has its source in the central highlands in the Wet Zone, is stored in reservoirs. On release it generates HEP, before transfer by canals, rivers and tunnels to the Dry Zone where it is needed to improve and extend irrigation.

Table 1.2 Mean monthly rainfall (mm) in Sri Lanka's Wet and Dry Zones

	J	F	M	A	M	J	J	A	S	O	N	D
Place A	97	37	30	70	63	16	17	32	48	244	411	267
Place B	280	135	138	234	246	215	203	201	189	373	354	341

Exercise

1 Calculate the mean annual rainfall at places A and B in Table 1.2. How do these rainfall amounts compare with the average for England and Wales? (Look back at page 14 before attempting to answer.)

2 What are the differences in rainfall amounts between the wettest and driest months at each place?

3 Illustrate the uneven distribution of rainfall during the year by:
   a Calculating the % of rain which falls in the periods February–May, June–September, and October–January for each place.
   b Use the % figures to draw two bar charts (one for each place).

4 Look carefully at the graphs you have drawn and answer the following.
   a Which place has the more uneven distribution of rainfall?
   b Which place is more likely to have a surplus of water which can be used for irrigation? Give *two* reasons to support your answer.
   c Which place is in (i) the Dry Zone, (ii) the Wet Zone?

5 Would you say that 'Dry Zone' is an accurate description of rainfall in the drier parts of Sri Lanka? How would you describe the pattern of rainfall in the Dry Zone?

The details of the Mahaweli Project are shown in Figure 1.33. There are five multi-purpose reservoirs in the plan. All, with the exception of Moragahakanda, will be complete by 1990. The Victoria Dam and Tunnel Project is the linchpin of the entire programme. It provides 210 MW of HEP, and the reservoir allows water to be diverted through an 8 kilometre tunnel at Polgalla near Kandy (Fig. 1.33) into the neighbouring basin of the Amban Ganga. A dam across the Amban Ganga at Botwatenna allows a second diversion through a tunnel into the Kala Oya basin. The finance and expertise for the Mahaweli Scheme has come from the World Bank and several developed countries, including the UK, Canada, Sweden and West Germany. Loans, technical assistance with irrigation work, and the construction of canals and roads, have come from Japan, the USA, Australia, Saudia Arabia, the EC and Kuwait.

On completion, the project will have created 265 000 hectares of *new* irrigated land and 100 000 hectares of improved irrigation on existing land. Irrigation will mean higher and more reliable yields (including double cropping, ie two crops from the same land each year), and permit a wider range of crops to be grown. It is hoped that Sri Lanka will not only become self-sufficient in basic food crops such as rice, but will also be able to export crops such as sugar cane, cotton, bananas, citrus fruits, mango and pepper. Food processing and packaging plants (eg for jams, chutneys, sauces, and the milling of rice) will be established in rural areas where they will provide much needed employment.

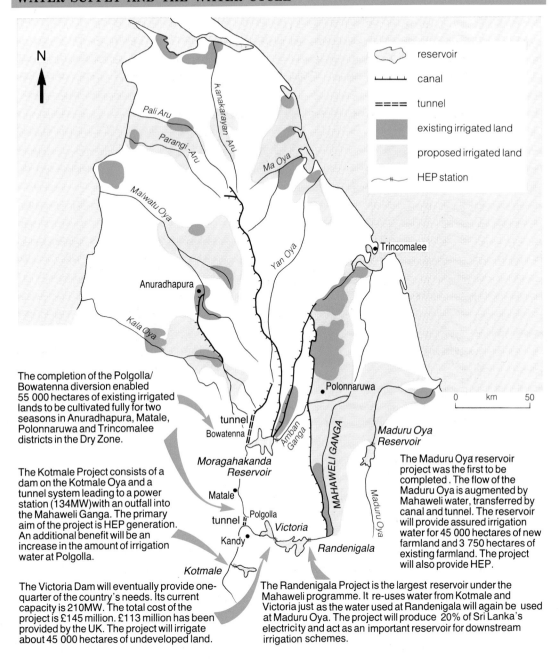

N

The completion of the Polgolla/Bowatenna diversion enabled 55 000 hectares of existing irrigated lands to be cultivated fully for two seasons in Anuradhapura, Matale, Polonnaruwa and Trincomalee districts in the Dry Zone.

The Kotmale Project consists of a dam on the Kotmale Oya and a tunnel system leading to a power station (134MW) with an outfall into the Mahaweli Ganga. The primary aim of the project is HEP generation. An additional benefit will be an increase in the amount of irrigation water at Polgolla.

The Victoria Dam will eventually provide one-quarter of the country's needs. Its current capacity is 210MW. The total cost of the project is £145 million. £113 million has been provided by the UK. The project will irrigate about 45 000 hectares of undeveloped land.

The Maduru Oya reservoir project was the first to be completed. The flow of the Maduru Oya is augmented by Mahaweli water, transferred by canal and tunnel. The reservoir will provide assured irrigation water for 45 000 hectares of new farmland and 3 750 hectares of existing farmland. The project will also provide HEP.

The Randenigala Project is the largest reservoir under the Mahaweli programme. It re-uses water from Kotmale and Victoria just as the water used at Randenigala will again be used at Maduru Oya. The project will produce 20% of Sri Lanka's electricity and act as an important reservoir for downstream irrigation schemes.

Figure 1.33 Mahaweli development scheme

About 130 000 families will benefit from agricultural resettlement under the programme. Each family is given one hectare of irrigated farmland, seed and plant material, a small house plot, and enough food until they reap their first harvest. All new settlements will be provided with a range of services, including schools, shops, a health centre, bank and post office, which will generate further employment. In addition there will be factories involved in the processing of agricultural products.

Finally, the generation of 566 MW of HEP will more than double Sri Lanka's existing electricity output and boost government plans for industrial growth, and electrification in the countryside. Through transfers of water between river basins,

Figure 1.34 The Victoria Dam: one of five multi-purpose dams, which form Sri Lanka's Mahaweli Development Scheme

the Mahaweli Development Scheme should eventually transform the Dry Zone into a highly productive agricultural area, which will attract new settlements, provide employment, and improve the lives of millions of Sri Lankans.

Exercise

1 Name the two main benefits to Sri Lanka from the Mahaweli Scheme.

2 Make a list of the advantages of irrigation agriculture using the following headings as guidelines: crop yields; range of crops grown; industries based on agricultural products.

3 In some parts of the Dry Zone, rural development through the provision of essential services (as well as improved agriculture and jobs in industry) will transform the lives of many people. What are these services, and how do you think they will affect people's lives?

Water resource issues

This section looks at two important *issues* connected with the water supply industry: the effect on the environment of the creation of a new reservoir; and the pollution of water resources. *Issues are subjects over which different people hold conflicting views causing them to disagree fundamentally.* As we shall see, these disagreements arise from the *values* and *beliefs* that individuals hold. Apart from helping you to understand these two issues better, this section aims to examine the values, beliefs and attitudes of powerful decision-makers such as Ministers of State, as well as ordinary people whose lives might be affected in some way. It should also help you to think about these issues yourself and express your own values, beliefs and attitudes towards them.

Building a new reservoir: a simulation exercise

A plan has been drawn up to build a new fertiliser plant at Storby, near the mouth of the River Eld. This will increase the demand for water from the river by an extra 30 000 cumecs per day. The water authority has the task of supplying this extra water, and has decided to build a *regulating reservoir* somewhere in the headwaters of the Eld basin. The purpose of the reservoir would be to even-out the river's flow: surplus rain in winter would be stored and released during the period of low flow in summer. The river itself would be used to transfer the water downstream, where it would be taken out for use by industry. Further advantages of the reservoir would be to guarantee water supplies in drought years, and reduce the risk of flooding in the Lower Eld Valley. After a thorough survey by the water authority's engineers and geologists, two sites for the reservoir have been shortlisted: Scardale, and the Eld Valley near Eldburn (Fig. 1.35). The effect of each site on the river's seasonal flow or *regime*, and the water resources made available, are shown as graphs in Figure 1.36.

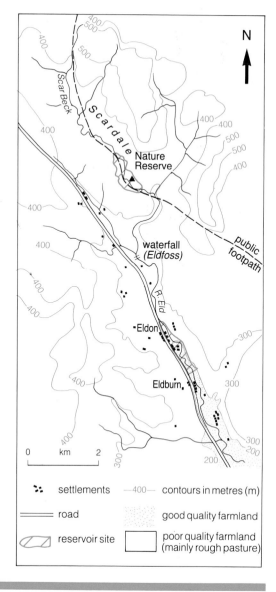

Figure 1.35 Potential reservoir sites in the upper Eld Valley

Exercise

Study Figure 1.36 and answer the following.

1 *Without* the regulating reservoir what proportion of the River Eld's flow occurs
  between a) December and February, b) June
  and August? Assuming that rainfall is evenly
  spread throughout the year, give two possible
  reasons for this difference.

2 During which three month period are *existing*
  water resources (ie without the reservoir or
  the fertiliser plant) fully used?

3 How much additional water could be supplied
  between June and August by a reservoir at a)
  Scardale, b) Eld Valley?

4 Which reservoir would have the biggest
  effect on the river's regime? Apart from additional water resources, describe any further
  benefits which would come from this modification of the Eld's regime.

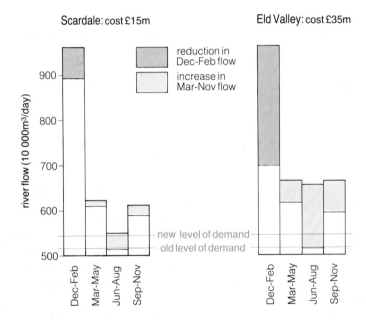

Figure 1.36 The effect of Scardale
and Eld Valley reservoirs on
river flow

Issue 1: where to site the reservoir

Exercise

1 Study the information in Figure 1.37 concerning the Scardale and Eld Valley sites,
  together with the map of the area (Fig. 1.35)
  and the graphs of river flow (Fig. 1.36). Then
  construct a table like the one on page 35.
  Compare the two sites by putting a tick
  against each factor for the site that you think
  is preferable.

2 Summarise the results from your table by
  writing a paragraph to compare the strengths
  and weaknesses of each site.

3 The table you have compiled might be a useful summary of the arguments for and against
  each site, but it says nothing about *how*

important each argument is. With this in
mind, rank the 'areas of impact' in your table
from 1 (most important) to 5 (least important). Try to explain why you chose your
rank 1 factor.

4 Find out how many students in your class
  placed each of the five 'areas of impact' first.
  Is there any agreement on which is the most
  important one? Divide into small groups with
  students who made a different first choice to
  you. Try to justify your choice to the other
  people in your group.

5 As Chairman of the water authority, write a
  report for the Secretary of State for the Environment, recommending either Scardale or
  Eld Valley as the site for the new reservoir.
  Explain clearly the reasons for your choice.

Area of impact	Factor	Scardale	Eld Valley
Environment	Damage to wildlife Damage to landscape[1]		
Economic	Cheapest site Loss of farmland Water resources[2]		
Recreation	Less access for walkers Tourist potential[3]		
River control	Better flood control Reduced drought risk		
Social	Loss of jobs, settlement and community		

[1] Includes the effects on Eldfoss and road building to the site.

[2] If you think that large water resources to meet possible long-term demand is preferable, tick Eld Valley. If you think that excessive resources for which there is no immediate demand are unnecessary, tick Scardale.

[3] If you are in favour of tourist development, tick Eld Valley. If you feel that tourism would further spoil the area, tick Scardale.

Scardale

Scardale is a remote valley, though it is popular with ramblers and hill walkers. There is a public right of way across the reservoir site. The site is of great scientific interest, and part of it is a nature reserve which protects several rare bog plants and insects. A reservoir at Scardale would destroy these rare species. Downstream from the proposed site is a spectacular waterfall called Eldfoss. If Scar Beck were regulated, then the impressive sight of Eldfoss when the river is in flood would be lost. Although the Scardale reservoir would satisfy the demand for water at Storby, if demand continued to increase then either the dam would have to be raised, or a second reservoir constructed. Opportunities for the development of recreational and leisure activities on the reservoir are somewhat limited, owing to Scardale's isolation.

Eld Valley

Eld Valley is easily accessible, with the only road in the area following the valley. The potential for recreational use of the reservoir is considerable (boating, wind surfing, fishing, picnicking, camping) and would attract large numbers of people from Storby at weekends. However, a reservoir would flood a large area of farmland on the valley floor, which provides hay for livestock in winter. In addition, seven farms would be flooded, causing some unemployment and large payments in compensation. The loss of these farms would also be a serious blow to the social life of the hamlet of Eldon, and the village of Eldburn.

A large reservoir in the Eld Valley would solve Storby's water problem until well into the 21st century. It would also regulate the flow of the River Eld, eliminating the risk of flooding, and water shortages in times of drought. However, there is no immediate demand for water resources on the scale of those available from the Eld Valley. Opposition to the new reservoir would probably be stronger at Eld Valley than at Scardale, owing to the greater impact that it would have on the lives of local people.

Figure 1.37 Information about reservoir sites. (See, also, photographs on page 36.)

Figure 1.38 Scardale

Figure 1.39 The Eld Valley

Issue 2: should a reservoir be built?

In the previous exercise you chose a site for the new reservoir on the assumption that the decision to build had *already* been taken. You may have felt that there was a need to *prove* the case for the reservoir. This exercise focuses on the issue of environmental well-being and jobs, and on whether a new reservoir should be built at all.

Exercise

1 Read the statements on pages 37–38 of people who have an interest in the issue. If a reservoir were built who would benefit and who would lose-out?

2 People's opinions or *attitudes* towards issues, are based on their *values* and *beliefs*. Values are what individuals *desire* to be true, and beliefs are what they *think* is true. For example, you may value the well-being of environment (no pollution, no damage to wildlife etc.) above the nation's economic growth, even though this may mean no improvement in your standard of living. However, at the same time you may believe that governments rate economic growth as being more important than the environment. Your combination of values and beliefs could result in an attitude which is opposed to developments such as the expansion of cities at the expense of the countryside, the removal of hedgerows in the interest of more efficient arable farming, and the dumping of low-level nuclear waste in the sea.

a) With the above ideas in mind, re-read the statements on page 39 and write down what you think are the missing values, beliefs and attitudes in Table 1.3.

b) Using all the information available, and balancing the economic, environmental and political interests, and human needs, work out your *own* attitude towards the issue of reservoir building. State clearly your own basic values and beliefs in relation to the issue.

c) Divide into small groups, and justify your attitude (in terms of your beliefs and values) to other members of the group.

d) Although everyone in your class has used the same information, it is likely that attitudes will vary. What are the reasons for these differences? How easy would you say it is to come to an agreement over an issue of this kind?

3 A number of people's lives will be directly affected by the decision to build or not to build the reservoir. Imagine yourself in the position of either:

a) an unemployed person with a young family to support, living in Storby, and eager to find work;

b) a pensioner who has lived all his life in Eldon, and whose cottage and village are threatened with flooding if the reservoir is built.

Write down your feelings in a letter to the editor of the *Storby Times*.

President of Chemco in a letter to the Secretary of State for the Environment:
'Dear Sir . . . we would prefer to locate our new plant in the UK . . . however if our profits are to be maintained it is essential that the go-ahead is given to build a new reservoir either in the Eld Valley or Scardale, and that its water be available within three years . . . otherwise we shall have no alternative but to look to the continent to expand our business.'

MP for Storby-on-Eld in a letter to the Chairman of the Democratic Party:
'Dear Nigel . . . it is vital that you put pressure on the Minister to approve the new reservoir in the Upper Eld Valley. You know how difficult the unemployment situation is up here and the poor showing of the party in recent local elections . . . and Storby is not the only marginal constituency in the region. What is needed is a decision to go-ahead, and quickly . . . whether it's Scardale or Eld Valley doesn't matter . . . we have a lot to do if we are to change public opinion before the next election.'

MP for Storby-on-Eld in a radio interview:
'We all appreciate the concern felt by residents in the Eld Valley to protect the environment, but at the end of the day employment has to come first. Last month's unemployment figures for Storby were the worst on record . . . every day, people in my constituency tell me that they cannot understand how the prospect of hundreds of new jobs could be lost for the sake of a few rare plants and creepy crawlers, let alone the odd acre or two of poor farmland . . . its got to be said that a lot of those who oppose the reservoir most strongly are commuters who live in the Eld Valley, but work in Storby, or who own weekend cottages in the area.'

Farmers' union representative speaking at a meeting in Eldon:
'Thousands of acres of farmland are being lost to industry and housing every year in this country, and yet farming is our most essential industry . . . we can't allow the countryside to be carved up like this any longer. Of course, we all know that unemployment in Storby is a national disgrace and it's time the government did something about it . . . but it's no solution to provide new jobs in Storby while farmers lose their livelihood in the Eld Valley.'

Engineering trades' union leader addressing a union meeting in Storby:
'We've got to get our priorities right . . . jobs must come first . . . many of you at this meeting know only too well the misery of life on the dole . . . it's all right for scientists and second-home owners to talk about protecting the countryside, but ordinary working class people round here can't even afford the bus fare, let alone a car, to get out into the countryside and enjoy it.'

University scientist in an article in the local newspaper:
'The plants and insects at Scardale are of enormous scientific value . . . this is an exceptional site, of national importance, which a recent independent study recommended should be protected at all costs. If Scardale cannot be protected, then no site in the country will be safe from big business and government interests. We must remember that we have a duty to protect the environment for future generations, and that although unemployment will not last forever, once Scardale has been flooded, its unique plants and insects are destroyed for all time.'

Local farmer at a meeting in the village hall:
'I don't want to sell my farm to the water authority so that they can flood it . . . I just want to be left alone to get on with my life . . . my family have farmed this land for six generations . . . those politicians and bureaucrats in Storby don't know what it means to us, and if they do they don't care . . . there are seven farms which would be destroyed by the reservoir and our community would never be the same.'

Representative of the Council for the Protection of Rural England at the same meeting:
'Any reservoir would completely spoil the beauty of the valleys. Like other reservoirs in this region, the reservoir would become a tourist attraction, with day trippers congesting the narrow roads with their cars . . . and picnic sites and water sports on the reservoir would destroy the peace and tranquility. If past experience is anything to go by, in a few years Chemco will probably close their factory and transfer their operations elsewhere, where profits are better. Then unemployment in Storby will be as high as it is now, and the Upper Eld Valley will have been despoiled for no purpose.'

Table 1.3 Values, beliefs and attitudes of persons involved in the issue of reservoir construction

Person	Values 'What is desired to be true'	Beliefs 'What is thought to be true'	Attitudes 'Positive and negative feelings/opinions on the issue'
Chairman of Chemco	Company profits are most important	?	Reservoir must be built either at Scardale or the Eld Valley
MP for Storby	Creating jobs for unemployed is most important	Unemployment will get worse unless the reservoir is built. Those opposing the reservoir are self-interest groups either recently moved into, or living outside the Eld Valley area	?
MP for Storby	Political power is most important	?	Reservoir must be built
Engineering trades' union leader	?	Without jobs people won't have the means to enjoy the environment	Reservoir must be built
Farmers' union representative	Protecting jobs of members is most important	If the reservoir is built farmers will lose their livelihood	?
University scientist	?	If Scardale is chosen a major environmental resource will be lost	Oppose the reservoir, particularly in Scardale
Local farmer	Human needs of the farming community are most important	?	Oppose the reservoir, particularly in the Eld Valley
Representative of the Council for the Protection of Rural England	Environmental well-being is most important	The reservoir would spoil the natural beauty of the region. The reservoir may only be useful in the short-term	?

River pollution

The use of rivers often results in their *pollution*. Polluted rivers are not only unpleasant to look at and be near, but they may pose a threat to human health. Severely polluted rivers are virtually lifeless, and in this state have little value as a resource: even with the most advanced methods of treatment their water may be unfit to drink, while they have few attractions for recreational activities like fishing and boating.

Exercise

Look at Figure 1.40 which lists several ways in which rivers are useful as resources.

1 Divide these uses into two groups – those which are likely to cause severe pollution, and those likely to cause little or no pollution.

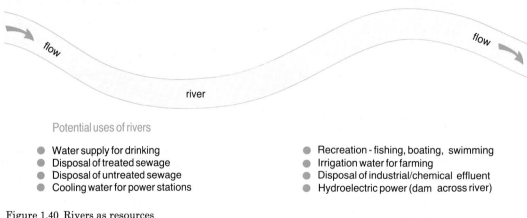

Figure 1.40 Rivers as resources

2 Draw an imaginary stretch of a river similar to Figure 1.40. Locate the different users of water on your diagram in such a way as to reduce to a minimum the conflict between them. For example, you would not locate a water supply intake downstream of an outfall for untreated sewage.

3 Does the distribution of polluting and non-polluting users on your diagram show any pattern? Comment in a couple of sentences.

We measure the level of pollution in rivers by their *biological oxygen demand* (BOD). The more polluted a river, the larger the number of bacteria present which remove oxygen from the water. As the levels of oxygen fall, the fish and other water creatures that cannot adapt to reduced oxygen levels (the least tolerant) are first to disappear (Fig. 1.42). Insects such as stonefly and mayfly larvae can only survive in well-oxygenated water, and soon disappear even at low pollution levels. On the other hand, bloodworms and rat-tailed maggots will survive in the most polluted rivers long after other creatures have disappeared.

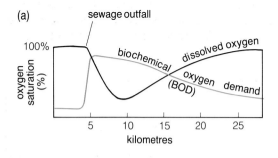

Figure 1.41a Effect of organic pollution on oxygen levels in a river

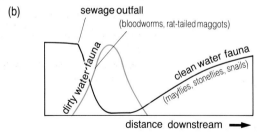

Figure 1.41b Effect of organic pollution on animal populations in a river

Exercise

Use Figures 1.41 and 1.42 to answer the following.

1 Describe and explain the changes in levels of oxygen along the river in Figure 1.41a.

2 At what distance downstream of the sewage outfall do fish start to reappear?

3 Which creatures are found in the most polluted stretches of the river?

4 Which species of fish will only thrive in clean, well-oxygenated water?

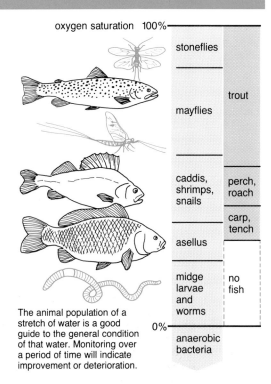

oxygen saturation 100%

stoneflies

mayflies

caddis, shrimps, snails

asellus

midge larvae and worms

trout

perch, roach

carp, tench

no fish

anaerobic bacteria

0%

The animal population of a stretch of water is a good guide to the general condition of that water. Monitoring over a period of time will indicate improvement or deterioration.

Figure 1.42 Animal tolerance of pollution

Rivers in the UK vary considerably in their levels of pollution. On the basis of water quality, four classes of river are recognised (Fig. 1.43). Class 1 rivers, such as the North Tyne, have water of high quality which is suitable for drinking and supports game fish such as trout and salmon. Class 2 rivers are only slightly polluted, but with advanced treatment their water can be used for drinking, and they support fish such as roach, perch and bream which are good for coarse fishing. The River Thames above Teddington is an example of a class 2 river. The badly polluted rivers are in classes 3 and 4. Class 3 rivers, such as the Exe below Exeter and the Ribble below Preston (Fig. 1.44), support few fish and their water is only suitable for low-grade industrial purposes (eg cooling water for power stations). Class 4 rivers, like the Mersey and Douglas in North West England (Fig. 1.44) are so grossly polluted as to be virtually lifeless, and are liable to cause environmental problems. Almost 10% of the total length of British rivers fall into classes 3 and 4. This may seem a small proportion, but it amounts to nearly 3000 kilometres: sadly in recent years there has been little or no improvement in this situation.

1A	1B	2	3	4

1A Waters of high quality suitable for drinking, supporting game fisheries and with high amenity value.

1B Waters of less high quality than class 1A, but used for the same purposes.

2 Waters suitable for drinking after advanced treatment; reasonably good coarse fisheries; moderate amenity value.

3 Waters polluted to an extent that fish are absent; may be used for low grade industrial abstraction; potential for further use if cleaned up.

4 Waters which are grossly polluted and likely to cause a nuisance.

Figure 1.43 Water quality of rivers and canals in England and Wales

Exercise

1 Draw three bar charts to illustrate the figures in Table 1.4. In which region is the problem of river pollution a) greater than, b) smaller than the national average?

2 With reference to Figure 1.44 name *three* rivers in South Lancashire which are grossly polluted.

3 Try to explain the changes in the levels of pollution along the River Ribble, and its tributary, the River Darwen.

4 Where along a river's course is pollution like-ly to be greatest? Give examples to support your answer from Figure 1.44.

Table 1.4 River pollution in North West and South West England

Area	Class 3 rivers as % of total river length in England and Wales	Class 4 rivers as % of total river length in England and Wales
England and Wales	8.0	2.0
North West England	15.2	4.8
South West England	5.7	1.0

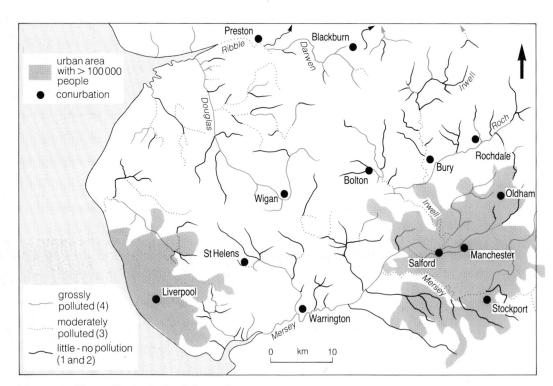

Figure 1.44 River pollution in South Lancashire

The causes of river pollution

The causes of river pollution are summarised in Figure 1.45. The effect of pollu-tants is twofold: first, pollutants such as sewage, farm waste and warm water from power stations reduce oxygen levels in rivers; and second, toxic chemical waste released by industries poison fish and other water creatures.

It is true that most pollution is legal: it is also true that most pollution could be avoided. But a clean river, which everyone agrees is preferable to a polluted one, might mean higher water rates and taxes to pay for better sewage treatment plants. It might also mean higher costs for many industries which would have to pay for more expensive ways of disposing of or treating toxic waste. In the long term this might even threaten jobs. The essential question then is how much are *you*

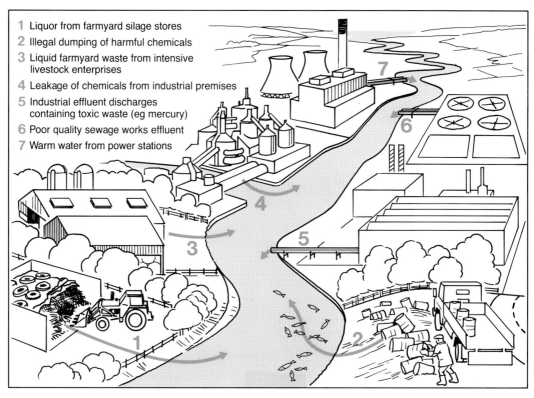

1 Liquor from farmyard silage stores
2 Illegal dumping of harmful chemicals
3 Liquid farmyard waste from intensive livestock enterprises
4 Leakage of chemicals from industrial premises
5 Industrial effluent discharges containing toxic waste (eg mercury)
6 Poor quality sewage works effluent
7 Warm water from power stations

Figure 1.45 Examples of river pollution sources

prepared to pay for unpolluted rivers? While polluted rivers are unpleasant, most people would probably prefer to put up with them, rather than pay higher taxes and risk jobs. At election time politicians find few votes for new sewage plants, however essential they might be!

Figure 1.46a Untreated sewage discharged into rivers is not only unpleasant, but a threat both to wildlife and human health

Figure 1.46b Chemical fertilisers used in agriculture are washed into streams and rivers, causing algal blooms, which de-oxygenate the water and kill aquatic life

Figure 1.46c Pollution from foam and detergents on the River Avon, Somerset

Towards increasing environmental concern ⟶

Values (What people *desire* to be true)	Economic considerations should always take priority over environmental considerations	We should, where reasonable, always seek to conserve environmental resources	Environmental resources should always be conserved, regardless of cost
Beliefs (What people *think* is true)	Rivers are instruments of economic policy to be exploited in pursuit of profit and higher standards of living Pollution of rivers is inevitable if living standards and consumerism are to continue to grow Only a small % of rivers are grossly polluted Environmental damage to rivers is temporary: when they are no longer required for disposal of effluent, they quickly recover, eg Tyne, Thames Rivers have always been polluted by human activities Without material wealth generated by industry, we could not enjoy environmental resources; the generation of wealth will always result in some pollution	Some pollution is inevitable, and tolerable, providing there is only limited damage to biological resources and to the beauty of rivers Most pollution can be prevented at reasonable cost, given the political and economic will of decision makers There should be no grossly polluted rivers because they: ● are a health hazard ● are unattractive ● restrict the resource potential of rivers for recreation and water supply The pollution of rivers stems from the power of business interests and political expediency on the part of government	Whatever the cost, pollution of rivers which in any way damages their resource potential, is unacceptable We have a duty, as custodians of the environment, not to damage environmental resources for future generations It is immoral to pollute rivers and destroy aquatic creatures Government supports industry which pollutes rivers to strengthen consumerism, capitalism and its hold on power River management schemes merely support exploitative attitudes by seeking to resolve conflicts, rather than tackle root causes
Attitudes (Negative and positive feelings towards issues)	Pollution is a price worth paying to sustain material wealth and standards of living (ie the status quo)	Pollution, could and should be reduced, even at the expense of some cut in living standards (reformist)	Pollution should be stopped, even if this means a drastic change in our way of life and a return to much lower standards of living (revolutionary)

Figure 1.47 The issue of river pollution

Exercise

1 South Lancashire is in the North West region, which has the highest levels of river pollution in England and Wales. South Devon is in the South West, the region with the lowest pollution levels. Using evidence from Figures 1.44 and 1.45 try to explain the levels of river pollution in the North West. Why should it be so low in the South West?

The issue of river pollution is looked at from three different viewpoints in Figure 1.47. The two extremes are: a) economic considerations always outweigh environmental ones, b) environmental considerations always have priority over economic ones. The third viewpoint is somewhere between these extremes.

2 Using Figure 1.47 as a guide, define your own values, beliefs and attitudes towards the issue of river pollution.

3 Write out your views in full, using the headings of 'values', 'beliefs' and 'attitudes'. Try to make sure that your overall view or attitude (ie your positive or negative feelings on the issue) is consistent with the values (what you *should* like to be true) and beliefs (what you *think* is true) that you hold.

4 Having prepared your views, divide into small groups and explain them to other students. Ask for criticism of your views and then consider whether you want to change any of your original ideas.

The River Rhine: 'the sewer of Europe'

Europe's greatest river, the Rhine, is often described as 'the sewer of Europe'. In November 1986, after the disastrous fire at the Sandoz chemical plant at Basel in Switzerland, 30 tonnes of pesticides, mercury and other poisonous chemicals spilled into the Rhine. Although the Swiss authorities were slow to alert their Rhineside neighbours, little could have been done to save wildlife in the river. So lethal was the chemical cocktail that drifted down the Rhine, that it poisoned virtually all wildlife between Basel and Mannheim (Figs 1.49a and b). Experts believe that it could take 30 years to restore life to this section. Further downstream the water supplies of many German villages were cut off, and precautions had to be taken to prevent farm animals from drinking polluted river water. Twelve days after the accident the pollution entered the North Sea, where it was carried northeastwards and was dispersed along the Dutch coast. Although the immediate danger quickly passed, there is still concern that mercury – one of the most harmful of all substances – could find its way into stocks of edible fish, and present a threat to human health.

Figure 1.48 Chemical works on the River Rhine at Leverkusen, West Germany. The chemical industry is a major source of pollution of the Rhine

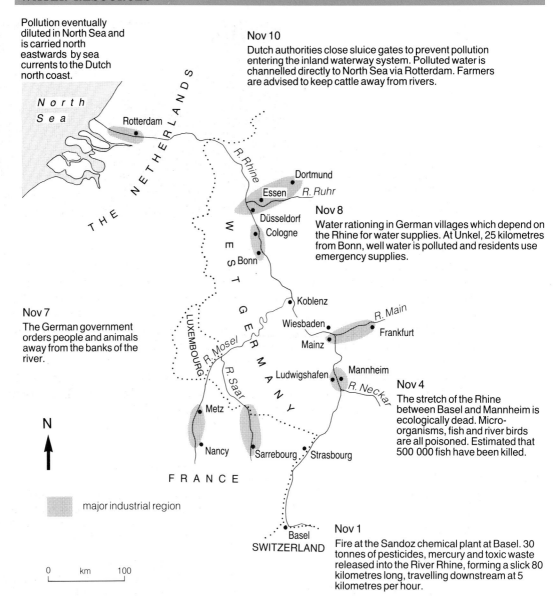

Pollution eventually diluted in North Sea and is carried north eastwards by sea currents to the Dutch north coast.

Nov 10

Dutch authorities close sluice gates to prevent pollution entering the inland waterway system. Polluted water is channelled directly to North Sea via Rotterdam. Farmers are advised to keep cattle away from rivers.

Nov 8

Water rationing in German villages which depend on the Rhine for water supplies. At Unkel, 25 kilometres from Bonn, well water is polluted and residents use emergency supplies.

Nov 7

The German government orders people and animals away from the banks of the river.

Nov 4

The stretch of the Rhine between Basel and Mannheim is ecologically dead. Micro-organisms, fish and river birds are all poisoned. Estimated that 500 000 fish have been killed.

Nov 1

Fire at the Sandoz chemical plant at Basel. 30 tonnes of pesticides, mercury and toxic waste released into the River Rhine, forming a slick 80 kilometres long, travelling downstream at 5 kilometres per hour.

major industrial region

Figure 1.49a The Basel chemical disaster and the poisoning of the River Rhine, November 1986

The problem of pollution on the Rhine is longstanding. It is particularly bad compared to other rivers because of the large number of industrial regions which line its banks and those of its tributaries (Fig. 1.48). The Netherlands, situated at the mouth of the river, has the most difficult problem as it receives everyone else's pollution. Each year seven million tonnes of salt, and smaller amounts of arsenic, copper, zinc, chromium and mercury reach the mouth of the river. In addition, there are huge quantities of sewage effluent and even some radioactive materials from nuclear power stations in France and West Germany. It is not surprising, therefore, that for several years Dutch inshore fishermen have noticed that an increasing proportion of their catch is diseased, or that the city of Rotterdam no longer draws on the Rhine for its water supply.

Figure 1.49b Dead eels taken
from the River Rhine in West
Germany following the accident
at the Sandoz chemical plant at
Basel in Switzerland on
1 November 1986

Controlling pollution on an international river like the Rhine has not been easy.
The first attempt to reach agreement between the five Rhineside states (France,
Luxembourg, The Netherlands, Switzerland and West Germany) was made in 1950,
but in spite of this the Rhine continued to carry a heavy pollution load. An
apparent step forward was made in 1976 when the Rhineside states agreed to limit
chemical pollution of the Rhine. However, many industrial companies continue to
treat the river as a convenient waste disposal unit (Fig. 1.50), and there is a lack of
any effective enforcement of the agreement.

It seems unlikely that there will be any determined cooperation among the
Rhineside states in the near future and, therefore, the Rhine will keep its unenvi-
able reputation as 'the longest open sewer in the world'.

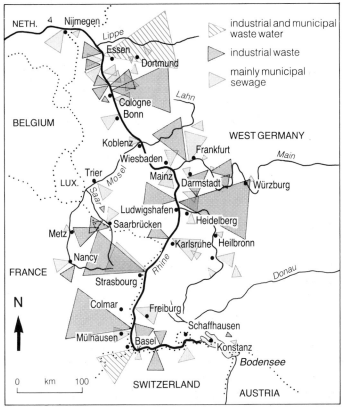

Figure 1.50 Pollution of the Rhine

Exercise

Read the extract from *the Guardian*
(Fig. 1.51) which comments on the accident at
the Basel chemical plant in 1986, which badly
polluted the River Rhine.

1 Name the following:
   a) Three main uses of the Rhine mentioned
      in the first paragraph.
   b) The five Rhineside states referred to in the
      extract.
   c) Three specific sources of pollution on the
      Rhine.

2 Which Rhineside state suffers most from pollution of the Rhine? Explain your answer and
   also mention any advantage that this state
   has when there is a pollution incident on the
   river.

3 What does the extract tell you about the
   attitudes of France and West Germany towards pollution on the Rhine? Support your
   answer with references to the extract.

4 How would you describe the attitude of the
   writer of the article towards pollution of the
   Rhine? Again, give specific details in support
   of your answer.

The river of no return

The Rhine is at once a road, a reservoir, — and a sewer. Like many a lesser "working" river (e.g. the Oder on the other side of Germany this week) it is perpetually exposed to pollution. For clean-up campaigns to make gains industry has to retreat (see the Thames and the Tyne and even the river Ruhr) — which does not mean we advocate unemployment as a cure for threatened waterways. At the upstream end of the Rhine are the Swiss, who are affected only by their own effluent ; at the mouth are the Dutch, who are affected by everybody's, even Luxembourg's ; in between are France and Germany, the two largest European industrial economies west of Russia. So when Swiss chemical companies, conveniently sited at Basle, right on the French and German borders with Switzerland, leak poison into the river and the Swiss fail to sound at once the international alarm, there is natural anger in long-suffering Holland. No country has a greater respect for water. But the rage in France and West Germany rings hollow.   In 1969 a boat, never found, dumped enough insecticide into the solely German stretch of the Rhine to kill 4,000 tonnes of fish. Ten years later the West German Hoechst chemical group came under fire for serious pollution and a state minister had to resign because his officials had fed the company with warnings of official action. For more than ten years the Dutch and Germans tried in vain to get the French to stop dumping waste salts from mineral mining and hot water from nuclear reactors into the Rhine : the Dutch went to the lengths of recalling their ambassador when the French refused to ratify an anti-pollution convention for the river. When a scheme finally got going, the French had the cheek to ask the other Rhineside states to share the cost (and they were soft enough to agree). Those are only the most spectacular cases. At least after this month's disaster the Swiss President himself and the Sandoz company offered compensation. That the polluter must pay is the second principle of dealing with pollution. The first is that prevention is immeasurably better than cure.

Even if the Swiss police had hit the panic button at once instead of 24 hours later, what more would the French and the West Germans have done ? What else could they do, apart from not drawing suspect water and standing on the banks to watch the 50-mile stain head for the Dutch border at a relentless five knots ? They have not said. The Dutch at least have one advantage in being at the end of the line : they may get the worst accumulation of pollution but they also get the longest warning (if any), and on this occasion seem to have used it wisely. With thousands of factories, power stations, sewage and water-treatment plants, port installations, fuel stores and boats with dangerous cargoes scattered along its 820 miles, the Rhine is at risk daily. People have often forecast its biological death after past ecological disasters, only to be proved wrong ; but its capacity to absorb such punishment must be finite, like every other natural resource on the planet. None of those living on its banks has the right to be sanctimonious or complacent. A properly protected environment comes at the same price as liberty — eternal vigilance. In fact for disasters like this latest one there is no cure except prevention. The world's busiest and therefore most threatened waterway needs the world's toughest protection treaty. Is this still beyond the wit of the five highly sophisticated Rhineside states ?

Figure 1.51 *The Guardian* leader article on the Sandoz chemical disaster, 14 November 1986

Exercise

The Great Lakes of North America (Fig. 1.53) have almost exactly the same area as the UK, and are part of a *drainage basin* equal in size to the UK and France combined.

1 Use the information in Figure 1.53 to draw a divided bar chart to show the relative sizes of the Great Lakes. Draw your graph to the same scale as Figure 1.52 and compare the sizes of individual lakes with England, Wales, Scotland and Northern Ireland.

Figure 1.52 Area of UK

2 Study Figure 1.53 to answer the following:
   a) In which direction do the Lakes drain?
   b) Which lakes are (i) least polluted, (ii) most polluted? Give three reasons to explain the pattern of pollution on the Lakes.

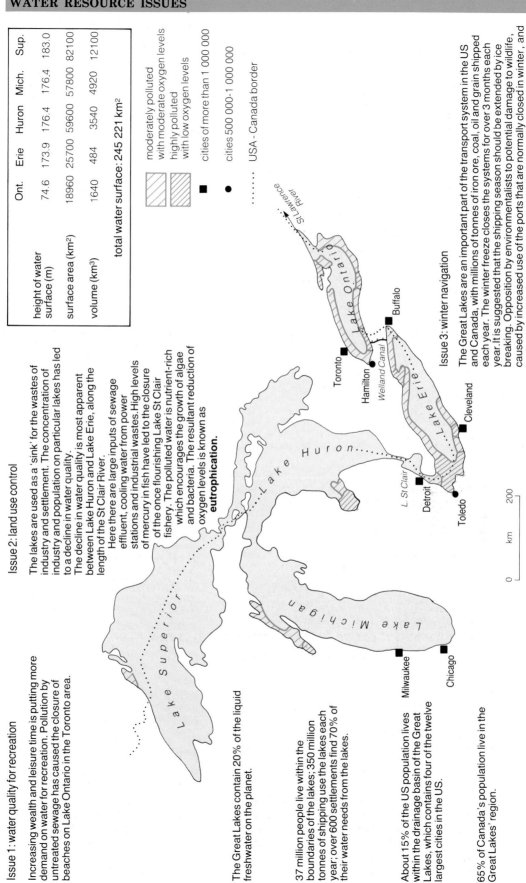

Issue 1: water quality for recreation

Increasing wealth and leisure time is putting more demand on water for recreation. Pollution by untreated sewage has caused the closure of beaches on Lake Ontario in the Toronto area.

The Great Lakes contain 20% of the liquid freshwater on the planet.

37 million people live within the boundaries of the lakes; 350 million tonnes of shipping use the lakes each year; over 600 settlements find 70% of their water needs from the lakes.

About 15% of the US population lives within the drainage basin of the Great Lakes, which contains four of the twelve largest cities in the US.

65% of Canada's population live in the Great Lakes' region.

Issue 2: land use control

The lakes are used as a 'sink' for the wastes of industry and settlement. The concentration of industry and population on particular lakes has led to a decline in water quality.
The decline in water quality is most apparent between Lake Huron and Lake Erie, along the length of the St Clair River.

Here there are large inputs of sewage effluent, cooling water from power stations and industrial wastes. High levels of mercury in fish have led to the closure of the once flourishing Lake St Clair fishery. The polluted water is nutrient-rich which encourages the growth of algae and bacteria. The resultant reduction of oxygen levels is known as **eutrophication.**

Issue 3: winter navigation

The Great Lakes are an important part of the transport system in the US and Canada, with millions of tonnes of iron ore, coal, oil and grain shipped each year. The winter freeze closes the systems for over 3 months each year. It is suggested that the shipping season should be extended by ice breaking. Opposition by environmentalists to potential damage to wildlife, caused by increased use of the ports that are normally closed in winter, and to changes in the temperature regimes of the lakes, has so far succeeded.

	Ont.	Erie	Huron	Mich.	Sup.
height of water surface (m)	74.6	173.9	176.4	176.4	183.0
surface area (km²)	18960	25700	59600	57800	82100
volume (km³)	1640	484	3540	4920	12100

total water surface: 245 221 km²

moderately polluted with moderate oxygen levels
highly polluted with low oxygen levels
■ cities of more than 1 000 000
● cities 500 000–1 000 000
······· USA – Canada border

Figure 1.53 Pressure on water resources of the Great Lakes

Figure 1.54a The skyline of Detroit as seen from Lake St Clair. The lake and its outlet – the St Clair River – receive sewage and industrial effluent from a population of 11.5 million. The result has been gross pollution of the lake and the disappearance of the once flourishing local fishery

Figure 1.54b Fish killed by pollution, on the shores of Lake Ontario, USA

Figure 1.54c Water transport on Lake Erie, with the city of Cleveland in the background. The Great Lakes are of vital importance to the USA and Canada for the transport of bulk cargoes, especially grain, iron ore, coal, limestone and petroleum

Cleaning up polluted rivers: the example of the River Tyne

The Tyne is the largest river in North East England, rising in the North Pennines and reaching the sea near Newcastle. Until 1980 there were 200 sewage outfalls on the river where it flowed through the Tyneside *conurbation*. Almost all the raw sewage produced by a population of one million people was discharged directly into the river. Not surprisingly, the Tyne was one of the UK's most polluted rivers: low oxygen levels along a 30 kilometre stretch to the mouth of the river (Fig. 1.55) meant that within the conurbation, the Tyne was almost lifeless. In summer, the smell of the river was a nuisance to people living and working nearby, while beaches along the coast at South Shields and Whitley Bay were polluted by sewage solids.

In the 1980s a major effort was made to clean up the river. It involved the building of a new sewerage system (Fig. 1.55) which stopped the discharge of untreated sewage into the river. Instead sewage was diverted along new pipelines

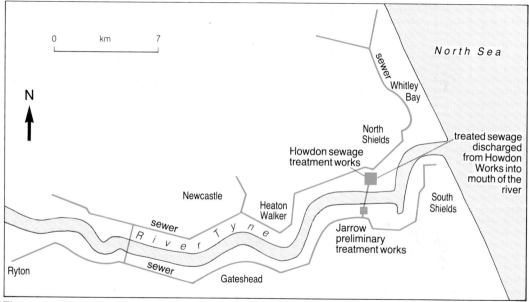

Figure 1.55 Cleaning of the River Tyne

Figure 1.56 The mouth of the River Tyne, near North Shields. Pollution of the river has been greatly reduced through the building of a new sewerage system in the 1980s

on both sides of the river to a new treatment plant at Howdon on the north bank. Here the sewage undergoes *primary* treatment, with the solids or sludge being separated from the liquid in huge sedimentation tanks. The solid waste is then taken by barge and dumped some 10 to 13 kilometres out in the North Sea, while the liquid waste is discharged into the river, just a few kilometres from its mouth. This simple treatment is sufficient to remove most of the pollution from the river, and already salmon and sea trout are returning in large numbers. This is a sure indication that the river, after 150 years of gross pollution, is at last returning to a healthy state.

Exercise

If you have studied the two previous sections, you might think that the sort of clean up that has been so successful on the River Tyne, could be extended to the River Rhine. Unfortunately, the Rhine presents a more difficult problem. Look back at the section on the Rhine and suggest three reasons why pollution problems on the Rhine are going to be more difficult to overcome.

The North Sea: remarkable natural resource or environmental dustbin?

The North Sea is a shallow, enclosed basin, surrounded by several of the world's most industrialised countries. It is an important resource for these countries accounting for $3\frac{1}{2}\%$ of the world's fish catch. It is also home to whales, dolphins and seals, and to millions of birds, including large numbers of wildfowl and waders that spend the winter around its coasts. Unfortunately, these same countries have too often used the North Sea as a convenient dustbin, for the disposal of sewage and poisonous wastes from agriculture and industry. The North Sea's capacity to absorb this pollution is limited, and today there is growing concern about its health and its future.

Causes of pollution

Pollution comes from several sources. One major source is the dredging and dumping out to sea of silt, from estuaries like the Elbe and Humber: silt from such estuaries is contaminated by heavy (polluting) metals and pesticides. Another source is fall-out of chemicals from polluted air over the North Sea. As we have seen, rivers like the Rhine, which drain into the North Sea, carry a heavy pollution load which includes dangerous pesticides, sewage, heavy metals, and nitrogen and phosphorus (used as fertilisers), washed from farmland. The UK is the only North Sea state which dumps sewage sludge into the sea: $7\frac{1}{2}$ million tonnes is dumped every year in shallow coastal waters, coating the sea bed in filth and releasing toxic chemicals and heavy metals into the sea. Other North Sea pollution sources include chemical waste burned at sea, garbage from ships, and oil spills from the North Sea oilfields, all of which add to the mounting problem.

Pollution of the Wadden Sea

Some parts of the North Sea are badly affected by pollution. The worst problems are found in the shallow southern water, and especially in the so-called Wadden Sea (Fig. 1.57). The North Sea currents spread pollution eastwards from the UK and from rivers like the Rhine, Schelde and Meuse (Fig. 1.57) and also trap polluted water from the Elbe, Weser and Ems in the Wadden Sea. The result has been a serious build-up of heavy metals, nutrients (nitrogen and phosphorus) and pesticides in the waters and sediments of the Wadden Sea. There is growing concern in West Germany, Denmark and the Netherlands about this pollution. These coun-

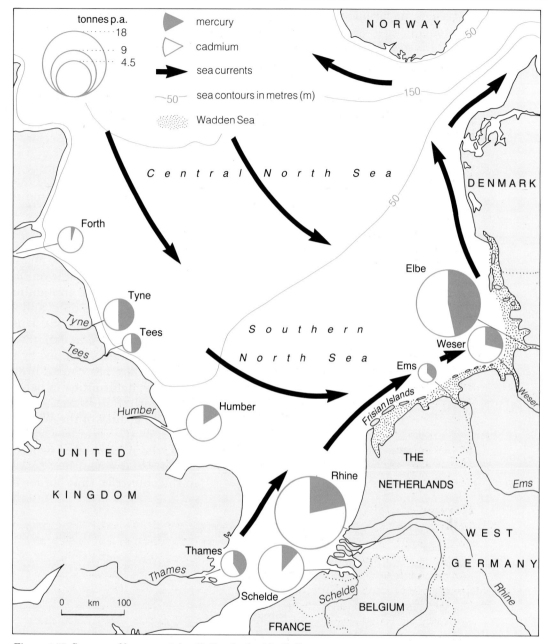

Figure 1.57 Sources of heavy metal pollution in the North Sea

tries see pollution of the Wadden Sea as an international problem (like acid rain), arguing that, in part, it is 'exported' from other countries, principally the UK.

However, pollution of the Wadden Sea is an issue which should concern all North Sea countries. In the first instance, it is, as the newspaper extract below illustrates, a distinctly beautiful place:

'The Wadden Sea is rarely more than 12 miles wide, bounded on the sea side by a chain of low, sandy, dune-bordered islands, the Frisian Islands, and to the coastal side by salt marshes, salt meadows and flat, reclaimed land. It is a hauntingly beautiful region where sea, land and sky seem to merge in an ever-shifting play of light and shadow, of greys and silvers, and faint blues and greens ... When the tide is up, the Wadden Sea is simply shallow, treacherous water. Six hours later it is wet, ribbed sand or mud interspersed with little

streams, apparently empty and silent but for the wind and the cries of oyster-catchers'.
The Independent, 24 November 1987

On more practical grounds, pollution should be stopped because the Wadden Sea is a vital nursery for so many different North Sea creatures. It contains abundant plankton, which is the food supply of thousands of tiny crabs, shrimps, worms and shellfish. They in turn are hunted by fish such as sole, plaice and cod which hatch in large numbers in the Wadden Sea. Some of these fish are, themselves, food for the seals and the nine million birds which breed, feed, moult or rest there each year.

This delicate web of life is today seriously threatened by pollution. Plankton and other micro-organisms absorb the poisons swept in on the tides, and these poisons are passed on to the shellfish and worms which consume them. These creatures may become so poisoned that they die, or they may in turn be eaten by larger creatures such as fish or seals. At each level the poisons become more concentrated. As a result fish develop hideous growths and diseases, and fishermen have to throw away up to one-third of their catch. Birds, and even the seals die. Eventually the contaminated fish may be eaten by people, and threaten human health (Fig. 1.58). This has already happened in Japan where consumption of fish poisoned by mercury and cadmium has caused brain damage in adults, deformities in babies, and even death. Pollution threatens more than the beauty of the Wadden Sea. It threatens the creatures which depend on it, the livelihood of fishermen, and ultimately the health of people living in the countries that border it.

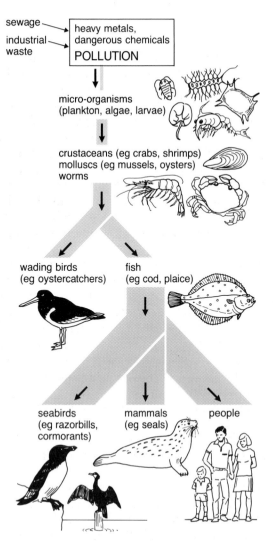

Figure 1.58 Concentration of poisons in food chains in the North Sea

Exercise

1 Use an atlas and name the countries which border the North Sea. Which two countries in this list are likely to suffer the least pollution?

2 Using the information given in Figure 1.57, which a) European river, b) British river, has the largest load of cadmium and mercury?

3 Give three reasons why the southern North Sea is particularly badly polluted.

4 The UK exports its pollution, while continental pollution remains largely in continental waters. Why is this?

Figure 1.59 A sludge boat on the River Thames. Millions of tonnes of sewage sludge are dumped around the UK's coast every year, coating the sea bed with filth, and releasing toxic chemicals into the sea

Figure 1.60 ICI's chemical complex at Avonmouth discharges a cocktail of pollutants into the Severn estuary, including heavy metals

Agreeing on a clean-up of the North Sea

Action to clean up the North Sea was agreed by the North Sea states in 1984. However, progress since then has been slow, largely because countries differ in their attitudes towards the problem (Fig. 1.61). Attitudes are determined by self-interest, values towards the environment, and disagreements about the effects of pollution on the North Sea. Thanks to its favourable geography, the UK is not greatly affected by pollution; the waters off the UK's east coast are for the most part deep, so that pollutants are quickly diluted. Furthermore, the easterly currents quickly remove the pollution and carry it towards the coastlines of West Germany and Denmark. Geography has been less favourable to other North Sea states, so that their coastal waters are more heavily polluted. Countries like West Germany, Denmark and the Netherlands, which receive their neighbours' as well as their own pollution, would understandably like to see stricter pollution controls applied to all North Sea states.

These issues were debated in London in 1987 at a conference on the North Sea. Some progress was made in uniting the two sides. The amounts of toxic substances and agricultural chemicals discharged by all countries into the North Sea will be halved by 1995, and the burning of chemical wastes at sea will end by 1994. The UK has also pledged to end the dumping of dangerous chemical wastes, mostly acids, into the North Sea by 1989. However, two other forms of pollution covered in this book – radioactive releases into the sea from the Sellafield nuclear reprocessing plant in Cumbria, and colliery waste-tipping in North East England – are to continue. The UK will also continue to dump sewage sludge into the North Sea because it is cheaper than either land dumping or converting it to fertiliser. But in the long term, dumping could be switched to the Atlantic Ocean. Under this scheme, sludge would be taken by tanker 1300 kilometres out into the Atlantic, and dumped in water 4 kilometres deep. Here it would sink to the sea bed and cause minimal pollution.

The London conference was hailed by the UK as a victory for commonsense, with real and lasting progress having been made. Other countries, though pleased that some progress was made, were less enthusiastic, and like the Germans believed that the conference had not gone far enough. The environmental group 'Greenpeace' was unimpressed, describing the conference as a wasted opportunity, with decisions postponed for another two years.

Exercise

Look carefully at Figure 1.61 and then think about your own values, beliefs and attitudes towards the issue of pollution of the North Sea. Summarise them in three short paragraphs.

Having thought about your own attitude towards this issue what are your views on the attitudes of a) the UK, b) the other North Sea states? Give reasons to support your views.

	Values	Beliefs	Attitude
Most North Sea states	The environment of the North Sea should be protected at *all* costs	The North Sea is severely polluted	Pollution of the North Sea should cease
		Pollution of the North Sea is the responsibility of all North Sea states	
		Action to prevent pollution should be taken before there is any proof of its harmful effects, despite the costs (ie nothing should be released into the environment if it might cause harm)	
		There should be the same pollution controls for all factories regardless of location (eg a chemical factory discharging toxic waste into the deep northern North Sea, should be subject to the same controls as a similar factory discharging waste into the shallow, southern North Sea)	
United Kingdom	The environment of the North Sea should be protected, but *not* at any cost	Pollution of the North Sea has been exaggerated: there are only localised problems, eg Wadden Sea	Pollution of the North Sea should continue
		Local pollution problems are the responsibility of the states directly affected	
		Most pollution comes from continental rivers such as the Rhine, Schelde and Elbe	
		No action should be taken until it has been proved that pollution has adverse effects	
		Pollution controls should be applied where they are most needed, ie southern North Sea	

Figure 1.61 The issue of pollution in the North Sea

Summary

Water is an inexhaustible resource, constantly recycled between the atmosphere and the earth's surface. Although 70% of the planet is covered by water, only a tiny fraction is fresh water, found in rivers, lakes and permeable rocks. It is this fraction which is vital as a resource for drinking, for agriculture, industry and energy production.

The demand for water in the UK, and the world generally, is rising rapidly. Unfortunately, the areas of greatest demand do not always coincide with the areas of supply. For example, in the UK the areas of highest population density are also the areas of lowest rainfall. In order to ensure supplies, regulating reservoirs are built in the uplands, groundwater resources are carefully managed, and river water may be used several times over (Fig. 1.62).

The development of water resources sometimes leads to conflict, especially when dams are built, causing valleys to be flooded and farmland, settlements and wildlife to be destroyed. Other issues surrounding the use and misuse of water resources are closely related to the pollution of rivers, lakes and the sea. This pollution greatly reduces the value of water as a resource, not least for recreation and leisure. While progress has been made in cleaning up many rivers, some, such as the Rhine and the Mersey remain grossly polluted. Until greater value is placed on a pollution-free environment, rivers, lakes and seas will continue to be used for the disposal of waste. Some will become lifeless and unpleasant to look at, and a few may even present a hazard to human health and well-being.

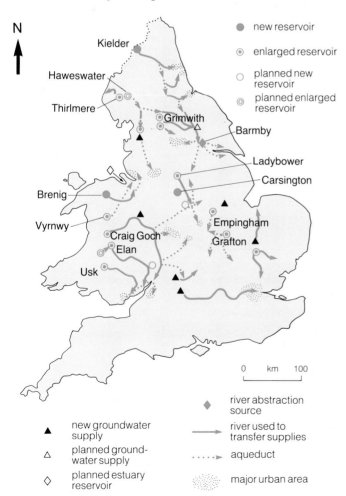

Figure 1.62 Water development in England and Wales 1981–2001

Further exercises

A

With the help of a labelled diagram, explain why water is described as a renewable and inexhaustible resource.

B

1 Describe and account for the distribution of reservoirs in Figure 1.62.

2 Outline the problems associated with the development of new reservoirs.

3 Explain what is meant by 'groundwater' in Figure 1.62.

4 What advantages do groundwater supplies have over surface supplies stored in reservoirs?

C

1 Name four activities likely to create a large demand for water.

2 Give two reasons to explain why water consumption has risen sharply in the UK in the last 30 years.

3 The problem of water supply in the UK is most acute in the south east.
   a) Give two reasons for this.
   b) Outline the efforts which are being made to solve the problem.

D

1 Name four ways in which human activities can pollute rivers.

2 For any one type of pollution:
   a) describe how it is caused,
   b) say why it is harmful to the environment,
   c) with reference to examples, explain how it is being controlled.

E

With reference to Table 1.5 answer the following.

1 On what % of reservoirs is a) fishing, b) sailing, c) water-skiing found?

2 Why is it unlikely that all of the recreational activities in Table 1.5 will be found on a single reservoir?

3 Refer back to the case study of Kielder and list some of the amenities which water authorities provide to promote recreation and leisure activities.

Table 1.5   Recreational use of reservoirs in England and Wales

Activity	Number of reservoirs
Fishing	484
Bird watching	275
Sailing	91
Sail-boarding	68
Sub-aqua	42
Rowing	15
Water-skiing	9
Total no. of reservoirs	530

Checklist of what you should know about water resources

Key ideas	Examples
Water is a renewable resource, constantly cycled between the earth's surface and atmosphere.	The water cycle comprises a number of stores (atmosphere, oceans, soil, permeable rocks, lakes) and transfers by evaporation, transpiration and precipitation between these stores.
Water resources depend on amounts of precipitation and rates of evaporation and transpiration, and are distributed unevenly at the global, national and regional scales.	Water resources are measured by the residual precipitation. In the UK water resources are greatest in the north and west, and smallest in the south and east. Unevenness in resources at the regional scale is shown in the Northumbria water authority area.
There are mismatches in the distribution of supply and demand for water in the UK.	The areas of highest demand are in the south and east, where water resources are smallest.
Water authorities in England and Wales are responsible for the management of water supplies.	Careful planning and management is needed in areas of limited resources, eg London, to ensure water supplies.
Water authorities increasingly provide recreational and leisure opportunities as well as water supplies.	Multi-purpose schemes such as Kielder, which in addition to supplying water to North East England, is Europe's largest water-based leisure complex.
The development of water resources can lead to environmental gains and losses.	Building of reservoirs for drinking-water or HEP leads to the flooding of valleys, loss of farmland and damage to wildlife. However, HEP is pollution-free, and reservoirs provide opportunities for recreation.
Misuse of rivers has led to widespread pollution.	River pollution, caused by industry, agriculture, sewage disposal, power stations etc is an international (eg River Rhine) and national (eg River Mersey) problem. River pollution results from values held by governments, industry and decision makers who place economic considerations ahead of environmental ones. Attempts are being made to clean up rivers (eg River Tyne and River Thames).
The sea is often used as a 'sink' for the disposal of industrial, agricultural and domestic waste.	Pollution of the North Sea by sewage, heavy metals, pesticides and fertilisers (eg nitrogen and phosphorus). Pollution is concentrated in the Wadden Sea, where it threatens wildlife (including fish stocks) and human health. The North Sea states are committed to reducing pollution, but countries differ in their attitudes towards the problem.
HEP requires specific physical conditions.	Conditions for HEP are favourable where rivers are large and powerful; precipitation is high and evenly spread over the year; lakes provide natural reservoirs; there are marked variations in relief. Favourable conditions are found in Norway and Sweden. They are largely absent in the UK.

Part Two

Energy resources

Why do we need energy?

Few resources are more essential than energy. We need energy for heating, lighting, agriculture, manufacturing, communications, transport – indeed for just about everything! In *developed countries* like the UK most of this energy comes from burning *fossil fuels* such as coal, oil and natural gas. However, in *less developed countries* we should not forget the importance of human and animal power, especially for agriculture, which still employs the bulk of the population (Fig. 2.3).

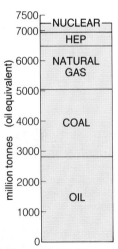

Figure 2.1 World energy consumption

Figure 2.2 Most DCs depend heavily on imported oil for their energy supplies. Oil is stored and refined in huge industrial complexes like Europoort in the Netherlands.

Energy resources may be *renewable* or *non-renewable*. Renewable resources include hydroelectric power (HEP), solar, wind, wave and tidal power and are inexhaustible. The non-renewable energy resources are the fossil fuels such as coal and oil. These take millions of years to form, so that once they have been used they cannot be replaced. Unfortunately the world depends very heavily on fossil fuels which are being rapidly exhausted. Indeed many experts believe that the world's reserves of oil and gas could run out within 50 years.

There are great differences between countries in the type of energy resources they consume (Fig. 2.5). The actual *energy mix* is determined largely by the resources available within individual countries. For example, the UK has a wealth of fossil fuels, and this is reflected in the importance of coal, oil and gas in its energy consumption. In contrast, France, which is badly off for fossil fuels, relies heavily on nuclear energy, fuelled by home-produced uranium ore. Where a country has to rely heavily on imported energy, such as Japan or Italy, oil, which is easily transported, is usually preferred to other fuels.

In the rest of this chapter we shall look in more detail at the production and consumption of coal, oil, gas and nuclear energy, and explore some of the issues concerning their use. HEP, which accounts for nearly 7% of the world's energy production, has been covered in the previous chapter on water resources.

Figure 2.3 Animal power still provides the bulk of the energy used by farmers in the less developed world

Exercise

Figure 2.4 shows how the consumption of energy in each continent varies with the level of technology (as measured by the proportion of scientists and engineers in the population).

1 Which continent consumes a) the least, b) the most energy? What differences are there in the level of technology between these two continents?

2 In a single sentence, describe what happens to energy consumption as the level of technology increases.

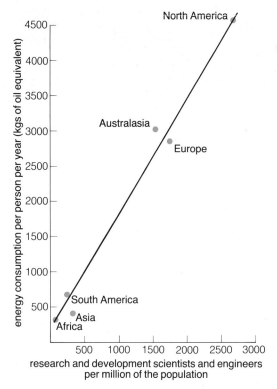

Figure 2.4 Energy consumption and level of technology

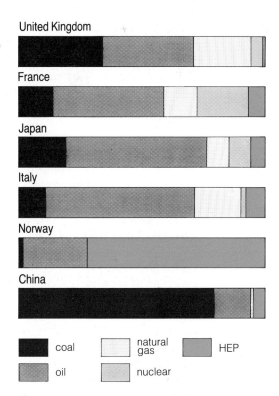

Figure 2.5 Energy mix in selected countries

Coal – yesterday's energy, or energy for the future?

Coal was formed over 250 million years ago from the remains of trees and other plants which grew in tropical, swampy conditions. Today it occurs in layers or *seams* which may be 1000 metres or more below the surface, and which can vary in thickness from a few centimetres to three or four metres.

World coal production

Coal supplies one-third of the world's energy consumption (Fig. 2.1) and ranks second to oil, as the world's leading energy source. Reserves of coal are huge and, at present rates of extraction, will last for more than 200 years. Coal is also widely distributed and, apart from South America, all continents have substantial reserves (Fig. 2.6). As a result, the amount of coal entering world trade is relatively small, particularly compared to oil. The principal exporters are the USA and Australia, while western Europe and Japan rely heavily on coal imports. Coal exported from the USA and Australia is produced at low cost by *open cast* mining (Fig. 2.7), and is transported cheaply in very large bulk-carrying ships. So efficient is this operation that in 1986, Australian coal was selling for £37 a tonne in western Europe, which was £9 a tonne cheaper than British coal selling in the UK at the time.

World hard coal production

USA	CHINA	USSR	POLAND	INDIA	UK	AUSTRALIA	WEST GERMANY	OTHERS

World hard coal reserves

ASIA (including USSR)	NORTH AMERICA	EUROPE	AFRICA	AUSTRALASIA

SOUTH AMERICA

Figure 2.6 World coal production and reserves

Figure 2.7 Open-cast mining in Indiana, USA. A giant dragline removes the overlying rock layers to expose a rich coal seam. This is the most economic method of mining coal, and helps to make American coal among the cheapest in the world

The UK coal industry

The UK has the largest coal industry in western Europe. Annual production is around 100 million tonnes, with 90% being *deep mined*, and the rest open cast. Reserves are estimated at 45 000 million tonnes; sufficient to maintain current production for another 300 years!

With the exception of the small Kent coalfield, the coalfields lie north of a line from the Wash to the Bristol Channel (Fig. 2.8). However, within this area there is an important division between the low cost *central* coalfield of Yorkshire, Nottinghamshire and Derbyshire, and the high cost *outer* coalfields of Wales, Scotland, North East England and Lancashire. More than half of the country's coal now comes from the central coalfield and, with the other coalfields in decline and major new coalfields about to come into full production at Selby (North Yorkshire) and Asfordby (Leicestershire), this trend is set to continue.

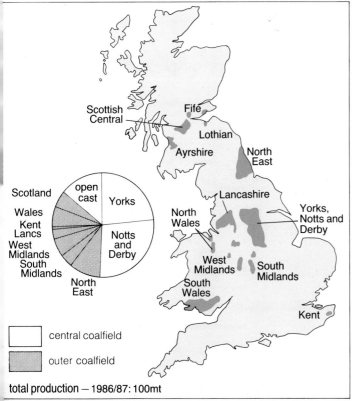

total production — 1986/87 : 100mt

Figure 2.8 UK coalfields

Exercise

1 Look at Figure 2.9. In which coalfield is productivity (ie, the amount of coal produced per man per shift) a) highest, b) lowest?

2 How does productivity in the central coalfield (Fig. 2.8) compare with the outer coalfields?

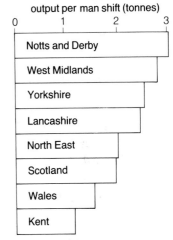

Figure 2.9 Deep-mined coal: productivity by coalfield

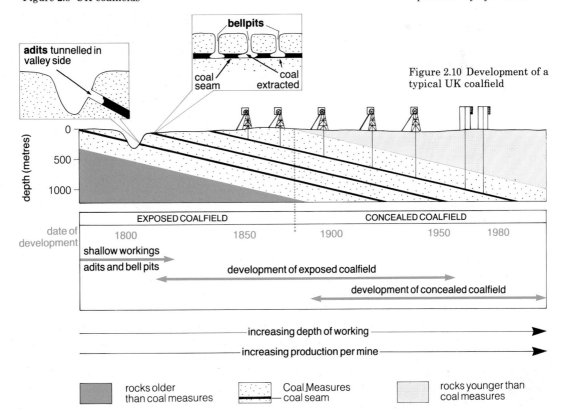

Figure 2.10 Development of a typical UK coalfield

3 The productivity, and therefore cost of mining coal is strongly affected by geological conditions. Study Figure 2.11 which shows three coalfields.

a What geological factors will make mining difficult in coalfields A and B?

b Name two advantages for mining in coalfield C. Why are coal seams b and c unlikely to be mined?

c Which coalfield is likely to have the highest productivity and mine coal at the lowest cost?

4 Although the national grid covers the whole of Britain, its density varies from region to region. Suggest a possible explanation for this. (Clue: look at Figure 2.12.)

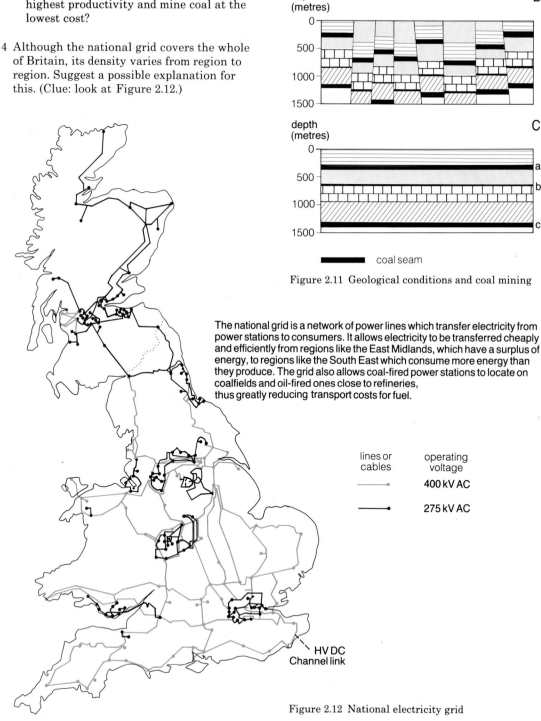

Figure 2.11 Geological conditions and coal mining

The national grid is a network of power lines which transfer electricity from power stations to consumers. It allows electricity to be transferred cheaply and efficiently from regions like the East Midlands, which have a surplus of energy, to regions like the South East which consume more energy than they produce. The grid also allows coal-fired power stations to locate on coalfields and oil-fired ones close to refineries, thus greatly reducing transport costs for fuel.

lines or cables	operating voltage
	400 kV AC
	275 kV AC

HV DC Channel link

Figure 2.12 National electricity grid

The central coalfield: 'powerhouse of the UK'

The central coalfield of Yorkshire, Nottinghamshire and Derbyshire extends over 120 kilometres, from the Aire Valley in West Yorkshire in the north, to Nottingham in the south (Fig. 2.13). It is the largest coalfield in the UK and contains several of the country's most productive pits. Kellingley colliery in Yorkshire (Fig. 2.13), known locally as 'Big K', was the first UK pit to produce 2 million tonnes of coal a year, while others, such as Thoresby in Nottinghamshire, and Shirebrook in Derbyshire, are not far behind.

The central coalfield can justly claim to be the powerhouse of the UK: it produces over half of the nation's coal, and, from the coal-fired power stations of the region it generates two-fifths of the UK's electricity. The largest of these power-stations is Drax near Selby (Fig. 2.13). It burns 30 000 tonnes of coal every day, or 11 million tonnes a year. Other very large power stations in the region are Eggborough, Ferrybridge, West Burton, Cottam and Ratcliffe (Fig. 2.13). The power stations are concentrated here because of the availability of cheap coal. Coal is transported from the collieries to the power stations in 1000 tonne trainloads by *merry-go-round* trains. These special trains, which are loaded and unloaded automatically while moving, run continuously in a circuit between the mines and power stations. Within the coalfield, the power stations are sited near to large rivers such as the Trent, Aire and Ouse, which provide water for cooling. Because the demand for water is huge, and supplies limited, massive cooling towers are

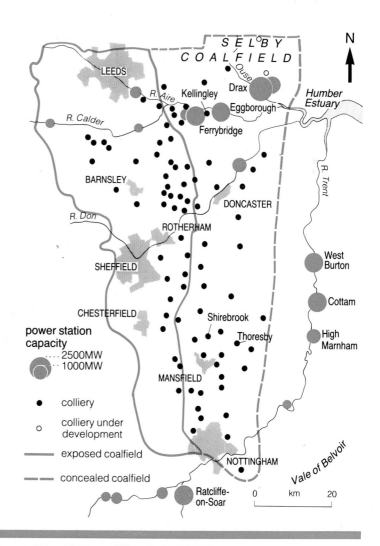

Figure 2.13 The Yorks, Notts and Derby (central) coalfield

needed to recycle the water. These cooling towers dominate the landscape over wide areas, and are familiar landmarks (Fig. 2.16).

Exercise

Look at Figure 2.14 which shows output and productivity of collieries in Nottinghamshire, Derbyshire, Leicestershire, Warwickshire and Kent.

1 How much coal is produced by a) the largest, b) the smallest colliery?

2 What happens to productivity (output per man shift) as output increases from individual collieries?

3 Eight collieries closed between 1983 and 1985. What features did these collieries share?

4 Although colliery A closed between 1983 and 1985, it was not typical of the other collieries which closed in this period. How was it different? Can you suggest one possible reason for its closure?

5 If you were chairman of British Coal, charged with making the coal industry as profitable as possible, which group of pits in Figure 2.14 would you a) earmark for closure, b) be prepared to invest in?

6 Six of the collieries which have *both* high output and high productivity are shown in Figure 2.15. How are the locations of these collieries similar?

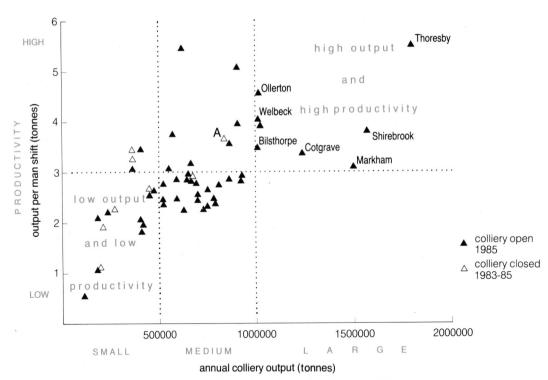

Figure 2.14 Production and output of collieries in Notts, Derby, Leicester, Warwick, and Kent coalfields

Exercise

Use Figure 2.15 to answer the following questions on the central coalfield in Nottinghamshire and Derbyshire.

1 Where on the coalfield did mining start? How did the distribution of mining change between 1863 and 1925?

2 How does the depth of mines change along the cross-section of the coalfield? What is the explanation for this?

3 How did the distribution of collieries change between 1947 and 1986? Demonstrate the changes by completing a table like the one opposite.

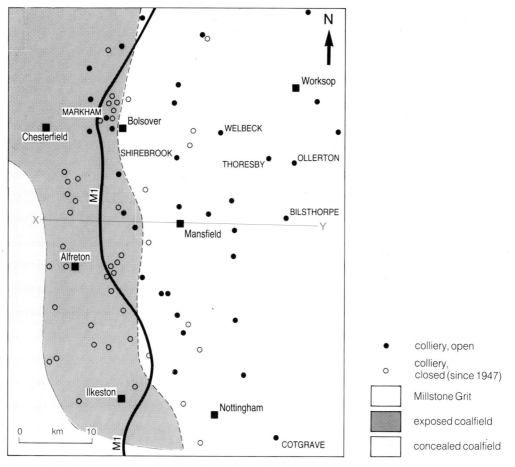

Figure 2.15a The Nottinghamshire and Derbyshire coalfield

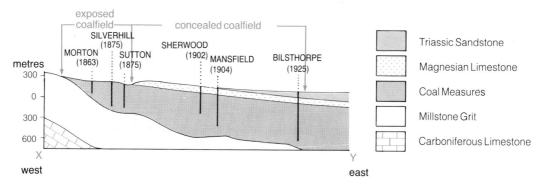

Figure 2.15b Geological section through the Nottinghamshire and Derbyshire coalfield

Distribution of collieries in Nottinghamshire and Derbyshire

	Exposed coalfield	Concealed coalfield
Number of collieries open in 1947		
Number of collieries open in 1986		

Figure 2.16 Ratcliffe-on-Soar power station. Note the large flat site, the river in the background providing cooling water, and the railway supplying the station with coal

The coal industry and the environment

Energy in abundance, but at what price?

Coal mining and electricity generation can have a devastating effect on the landscape in long-established mining areas. One such area is the Lower Aire Valley (Fig. 2.17) in Yorkshire, where mining has gone on for over a century. Here the landscape is disfigured by *spoil heaps*, widespread *subsidence* and open-cast workings. Moreover, several large power stations, with their cooling towers, smoke-stacks and transmission lines dominate the landscape, and create a major problem of waste disposal by producing millions of tonnes of ash each year.

The worst mess has resulted from the shallow spread of colliery waste on swamp land created by mining subsidence. In the area between Allerton and Ferrybridge (Fig. 2.17) land on the River Aire's flood plain has subsided below the level of the water table, forming a series of lagoons. In this same area, large-scale tipping of ash from Ferrybridge power station has occurred, creating a scene of desolation. Furthermore, since 1944 over twenty open-cast sites have been worked in the valley. At existing sites, towering heaps of spoil are visible for miles around.

However, the effects of mining are not always bad. Spoil heaps are being reclaimed by British Coal, and either vegetated or covered in top soil and returned to agricultural use. Several lagoons form valuable wetlands for waterfowl, and some are protected as nature reserves. Even open-cast mining has its positive side. First, its effects are temporary, with sites only being in use for three or four years. Second, it often takes place on land already spoiled by mining and so gives the opportunity to remove old eyesores from the landscape. And finally, during the restoration of these sites, the old open-cast mines are filled with spoil from nearby collieries.

The most pressing problem in the Lower Aire Valley is the disposal of ash from the three big power stations. At Gale Common alongside the M62 (Fig. 2.17) a landscaped hill 57 metres high, is being constructed from ash, piped as a slurry from Eggborough and Ferrybridge. A similar man-made hill is being created at Drax, and is gradually being reclaimed and restored to farming and forestry.

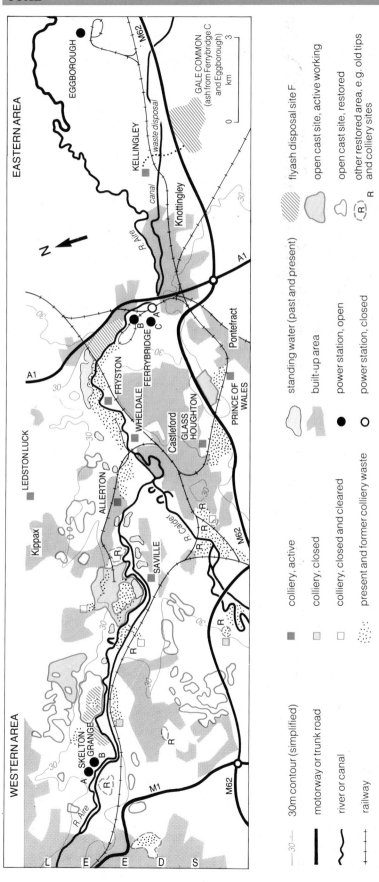

Figure 2.17 Energy and the landscape in the Lower Aire Valley

Figure 2.18 This lagoon near Castleford, formed by mining subsidence, is now a nature reserve

Figure 2.19 Mining spoil at Cwm Colliery, South Wales

Figure 2.20 A huge open cast site between Leeds and Castleford. In the distance, lagoons formed by mining subsidence, dominate the flood plain of the River Aire

Exercise

Look at the photographs which show the effects of mining and electricity generation on the landscape (Figs 2.19 and 2.20).

1 Describe your feelings towards the landscapes disfigured by those economic activities.

2 Coal provides 40% of the UK's energy needs, employs 130 000 people, and supports whole communities. In view of this, do you think we should allow the sort of environmental damage shown here? Write down your views and discuss them with others in your class.

3 Study the two photographs in Figure 2.21:
   a Describe the landscape before and after restoration.
   b Describe two advantages of tip restoration for the local community.
   c From the evidence of Sherburn Hill, how successful is modern tip restoration? Does your answer alter the view you expressed in question 2. If so, how?

Figure 2.21 Sherburn Hill, a former mining village in East Durham dating back to 1835. The photograph on the right shows the landscape after the reclamation of the tip in 1969

Coalfields for the twenty-first century

The development of new coalfields like Selby, on *greenfield* sites in rural areas, is controversial. Strong opposition comes from local farmers, residents and conservationists who have little to gain, and much to lose from the coalfield. They may force the coal industry to modify its plans, and to show greater concern for the environment than it would in a long-established mining area like South Wales or Durham.

Selby, which is Europe's largest new coalfield, is also one of the best farming areas in the UK. Farmers here were concerned that the new coalfield would mean a loss of farmland, subsidence, and damage to drainage. Subsidence could have very serious effects, as the Selby area is only a few metres above sea level, and even a small fall in land level could result in disastrous flooding from the River Ouse. Further objections were that subsidence would cause damage to buildings in the market town of Selby, including its ancient abbey, and to the main London–Edinburgh railway line which crossed the coalfield between Doncaster and York.

Because of these objections, British Coal's plans were the subject of a public enquiry, where all sides were able to express their views. In 1976 the government eventually gave the go-ahead for the Selby project, but imposed strict conditions for the protection of the environment. For instance, subsidence was not to exceed one metre, which meant that only about half of the coal reserves could be extracted. Mining under the town of Selby was prohibited, and all pit-head gear had to be carefully landscaped. Finally, British Coal had to meet the cost of diverting the main railway line around the western edge of the coalfield (Fig. 2.22).

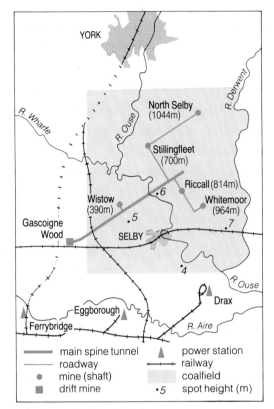

Figure 2.22 Selby coalfield

The Selby coalfield comprises five shaft mines, linked by two parallel spine tunnels to one large drift mine at Gascoigne Wood. All the coal is brought to the surface by conveyor belts at the drift mine. The purpose of the five shaft mines is to provide access to the coalfield for men and materials.

Reserves of coal are 2000 mt but planning permission has only been given to extract 350 mt. Annual production will be 10 mt, with productivity 12.5 t per man shift - five times the UK average!

Coal seams dip towards the north east. Thus the mines become progressively deeper in this direction. The Barnsley seam varies in thickness from 2 to 3.25 metres and has suffered little faulting. This permits high rates of production.

Thick seams and high quality coal mean that very little rock waste will be brought out. Hence there is no need for washeries to separate coal from shale and dirt and there will be no spoil tips on the coalfield.

The visual impact of the coalfield is small. Because no coal surfaces at any of the five shaft mines, there is no need for coal handling facilities and rail sidings. The head gear of the shaft mines is carefully landscaped and the drift mine is screened by trees.

Figure 2.23 Gascoigne Wood drift mine, Selby. The entire output of the Selby coalfield surfaces here, and is transferred by rail to nearby power stations

Figure 2.24 Wistow mine on the Selby coalfield. The pit head gear has been designed to minimise its impact on the landscape

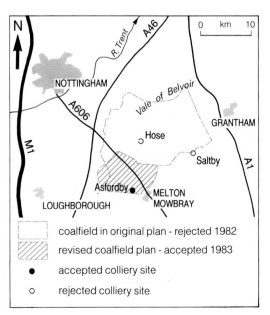

Figure 2.25 North East Leicester (Vale of Belvoir) coalfield

British Coal encountered similar problems in the new North East Leicestershire coalfield, where it planned to develop three pits with a combined output of 7 million tonnes a year. Here the main issue was the intrusion of mining, with its pit-head gear, coal-separating plants, heavy lorries and tips, into the picturesque Vale of Belvoir (Fig. 2.25). The public enquiry's recommendations in 1979 largely favoured the objectors: British Coal was allowed to develop only a single mine – at Asfordby – and this lay outside the sensitive Vale of Belvoir, on a site of little value, opposite an old iron works.

Acid rain: the silent crisis

The rain, which once was pure, is today sour and acid. On occasions scientists have recorded rain which is even sourer than vinegar! Although the problem of acid rain was first recognised more than a century ago, only recently has it been shown to cause serious damage to the environment. Today acid rain is an environmental issue of international importance.

Acid rain is caused by air pollution. The two main ingredients are sulphur dioxide and nitrogen oxides emitted by power stations and vehicle exhausts (Fig. 2.26). In other words, acid rain is largely an unwanted by-product of the energy industries, especially electricity generation through the burning of coal.

The significance of acid rain is the serious harm that it is doing to the environment. Forests throughout Europe and North America are dying; thousands of lakes and rivers are lifeless as their waters are acidified; and the stonework of hundreds of historic buildings in Europe is being eaten away at an alarming rate.

Scientists believe that the extent of damage caused to forests and wildlife by acid rain depends on: a) the amount of rain, and b) the nature of the underlying rocks. The more rain, the more acid is dumped on an area. When rocks are hard and impermeable like granite, and run-off is rapid, the water is likely to remain acidic, whereas in areas of permeable rocks, such as chalk or limestone, the acid water can be neutralised.

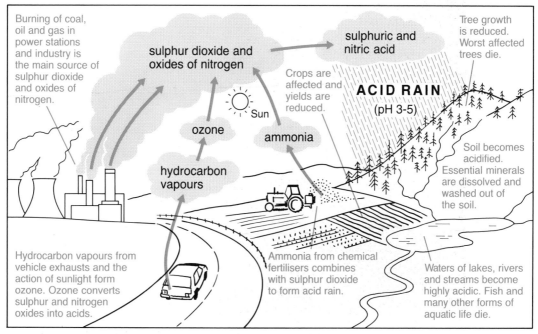

Figure 2.26 Sources of atmospheric pollution and acid rain

Table 2.1 The damaging effects of acid rain

Forests	Acid rain washes from the soil essential minerals needed by trees, and damages their leaves and needles. Weakened and exposed to attack by insects and fungi, vast areas of forest in West Germany, Switzerland, Austria, Scandinavia and the UK are dying (Fig. 2.27).
Lakes and rivers	Fish and other forms of aquatic life cannot survive in highly acidic water. Fish die because: a) acid water kills the insects which are the food supply for young fish, b) acid rain washes large amounts of aluminium from the soil into rivers and lakes where it suffocates the fish. In Sweden 18 000 lakes have been poisoned by acid rain, and 4000 are virtually fishless. The problem is also severe in many Scottish lochs, and in the smaller lakes of the English Lake District and North Wales. As insect and fish life disappear, other animals which depend on them, such as the dipper, the osprey and the otter, are threatened.
Buildings	In the cities, acid rain attacks the stonework of buildings and speeds up the normal weathering processes (Fig. 2.28). The rapid decay of the stonework on historic buildings such as Westminster Abbey and York Minster is causing great concern. For instance at St Paul's Cathedral some stonework is being destroyed at the rate of $2\frac{1}{2}$ centimetres every hundred years.

Figure 2.27 Die-back on a beech tree as a result of acid rain, Maisemore, N.W. Gloucester

Figure 2.28 A stone figurine on Gloucester cathedral, England, badly weathered by acid rain

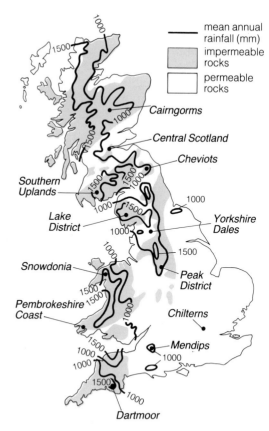

Figure 2.29 Rainfall, rocks and acid rain

Exercise

In this exercise you are asked to find out where in Britain forests and wildlife are most at risk from acid rain. Start by looking at Figure 2.29 and Table 2.2

1 Table 2.2 shows rainfall acidity for combinations of rock type and mean annual rainfall. Use this table, and Figure 2.29 to find out the likely acidity of rainfall at the places named in Figure 2.29.

Table 2.2 Rainfall acidity

Mean annual rainfall	Impermeable rocks	Permeable rocks
more than 1500 mm	High	Medium
1000–1500 mm	High	Low
less than 1000 mm	Medium	Low

2 In general terms, which parts of Britain are likely to suffer most from acid rain?

The areas most affected by acid rain are the uplands of northern and western Britain. As these are the main forest-growing areas, there is particular concern about the acid rain problem.

However, there are no easy solutions. The root cause of the problem is our demand for the large amounts of energy which we require in order to sustain our high standard of living. Nonetheless, many western countries are taking some action. For instance, all European Community (EC) countries, with the exception of the UK, have agreed to cut their output of sulphur dioxide from power stations

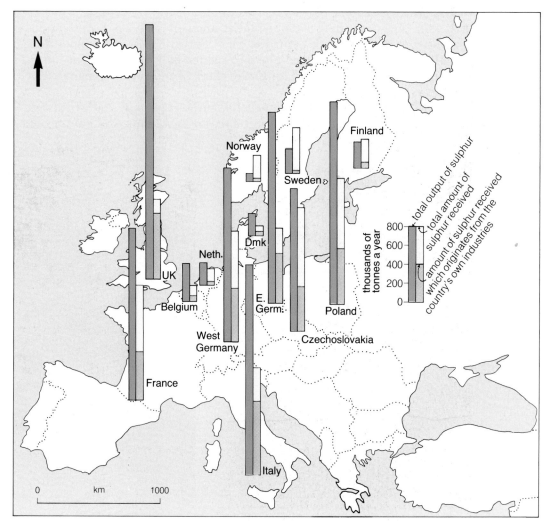

Figure 2.30 Atmospheric pollution by sulphur in Europe

by 30% by 1995. The UK has been unwilling to join the so-called '30% club': 70 million tonnes of coal are burned in UK power stations every year (much more than any other EC country), and the cost of reducing pollution would be enormous.

Exercise

Study Figure 2.30 which shows output of sulphur (a major cause of acid rain) from several European countries.

1 Which country has the largest output of sulphur?

2 Norway has the lowest output of sulphur. Look at pages 25–28 and give two reasons why Norway produces so little sulphur pollution.

3 Which countries receive more sulphur than they produce? What do you notice about the origin of the sulphur received in these countries?

4 The amount of sulphur received in the UK is relatively small considering the scale of its sulphur output. Can you explain this? (Clue: prevailing winds)

The rest of Europe has grown increasingly impatient with the UK's attitude towards the problem. The Scandinavians in particular feel aggrieved. They are situated downwind of the UK power stations, which they blame for the acid rain that is destroying their forests and wildlife. For the time being, all that they can do is to pour lime onto their poisoned lakes and soil (Fig. 2.31), in the hope of neutralising the acidity. Meanwhile, the Central Electricity Generating Board (CEGB) has at last announced plans to reduce pollution levels at four of its power stations, although this falls a long way short of the action demanded by the UK's European neighbours.

Acid rain threatens all countries, and, without prompt and worldwide action, it could become not just a problem, but a major environmental catastrophe before the end of the century.

Exercise

1 Explain why acid rain is an *international* issue.

2 Assuming that the main cause of acid rain is pollution from power stations (Figure 2.26 shows that there are other causes), what action, if any, do you think the UK government should take? Would you support a proposal to reduce pollution, if it meant a 20–30% increase in your electricity bill? Write down your views and discuss them in class with other students.

Figure 2.31 Snow being neutralised with lime before the spring thaw in Sweden. Meltwater is more acidic than rain and can cause severe damage to soils and the forests which depend on them

Coal: not just a source of energy, but a way of life

Between March 1984 and March 1985, the UK coal industry experienced its longest and most bitter strike (Fig. 2.32). The central issue was pit closures. British Coal, concerned about its huge losses, decided it must close some of its most unprofitable pits. The National Union of Mineworkers (NUM) opposed any closures that meant job losses for its members and contraction of the coal industry. Eventually, after a whole year on strike, the miners accepted defeat. Two years after the end of the strike, nearly 40 pits had closed and 50 000 miners had left the industry, but productivity had risen to record levels and losses had been cut sharply.

Figure 2.32 Violence flares on the picket line at Tilmanstone Colliery, Kent, during the miners strike 1984–85

Table 2.3   Pit closures: the economic arguments

For closure	Against closure
Closure of unprofitable pits means cheaper coal for the CEGB and therefore cheaper electricity for industry and private householders.	Pit closures create unemployment. The unemployed have to be supported by the taxpayer in social security benefits.
The taxpayer cannot be expected to pour money into 'clapped-out' pits. The money saved could be invested profitably elsewhere.	Even if redundant mineworkers are transferred to other pits, young school leavers will not have the chance of working in the coal industry.
	Once closed, pits cannot be re-opened. Any remaining reserves will be lost. Such reserves could be crucial once North Sea oil and gas are exhausted.
	A pit may be unprofitable today, but oil shocks like those of 1973 and 1979 (see page 87) could overnight transform loss-making pits into profitable ones.

The contraction of mining in the outer coalfields such as Durham and South Wales has been massive in the post-war years (Fig. 2.33). Decline has resulted partly from exhaustion of reserves, and partly from poor geological conditions which have made mining unprofitable. The effects of decline, as we shall see, have not just been economic.

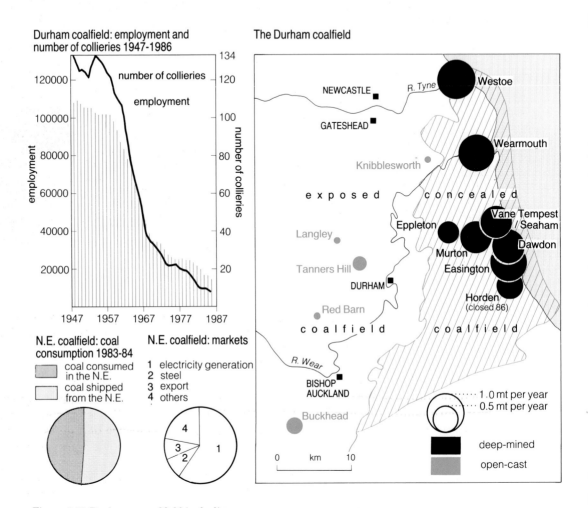

Figure 2.33 Durham: a coalfield in decline

Exercise

1 Large scale mining in Durham began on the exposed coalfield in the early nineteenth century. Where is deep mining concentrated today?

2 In view of the present location of the mining industry, what are its likely prospects in the long-term?

3 What type of mining survives on the exposed coalfield? Why do you think it is found there?

4 What is the main market for Durham coal?

5 Between 1947 and 1957 the rate of pit closures greatly exceeded the rate of job losses. What does this tell you about many of the collieries in Durham 40 years ago?

6 Compare the number of collieries and employment in mining in Durham in 1947 with the situation today.

Exercise

Read through the following description of Easington, a mining village on the coast in County Durham.

'Unlike many neighbouring villages named after a colliery, Easington still has its pit: a million-tons-a-year monster, employing nearly 2,600 men. It stands at the bottom of rows of coal board houses that look like a set from Coronation Street . . . unemployment locally is 18.5%, but in the older villages that have lost their collieries it goes up to 40%. There is a slow strangulation of the community; first the pit goes and then the shops, but most people cannot uproot . . . some of the shops are going already in Easington. "Lease for sale" signs stud the main street at regular intervals . . . And there is a waiting list of 300 people who would like to go 1,500 feet below the North Sea.'
The Times 8 August 1984

Figure 2.34 The mining village of Easington on the Durham coast

1 What has happened to mining villages in Durham which have lost their pits in the past?

Do you think that people should move to find employment?

2 If people lose their jobs, why do you think that it is often difficult for them to 'uproot' and take a job in another part of the country?

3 Comment on the statement that 'there is a waiting list of 300 people who would like to go 1500 feet below the North Sea'.

Throughout the coalfields, there are many settlements where mining is virtually the only source of jobs (Fig. 2.35). These communities have always been tightly-knit, with family ties and friendships that have been strengthened through working in a hard, dirty and often dangerous industry. The closure of a pit is likely to have devastating effects on such communities (Fig. 2.36). Shops, working men's clubs, pubs and community centres disappear, and families may be split as people are forced to leave to find jobs. Usually it is the younger people who move away, leaving behind an ageing population. Slowly the community is destroyed; a situation which many may regret as much as losing their jobs at the pit.

Exercise

Imagine that you are a miner in a pit that British Coal regards as unprofitable, and wants to close. Before the final decision is taken, an independent review body will look into the economic and social effects of closure, and may recommend that the pit remains open. Write a letter to this body, arguing the case against closure, and in particular describing the effects that closure will have on the community.

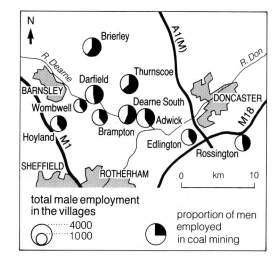

Figure 2.35 Mining villages in South Yorkshire: coal mining as a proportion of male employment

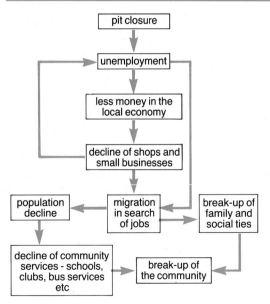

Figure 2.36 Pit closure and the spiral of decline in mining villages

Figure 2.37 Colliery waste tipping on the coast at Easington, County Durham. The lorry in the foreground is part of a small industry that salvages coal, dumped with the spoil, into the sea.

'Slag heaps on sea': the issue of colliery waste tipping on the Durham coast

The effects of tipping of colliery waste along the Durham coast over the last 80 years are appalling. Along a 10 kilometre stretch of coastline between Seaham and Easington the sea is filthy, the beaches are black, and virtually all marine life has been eliminated from the shore. This, the most polluted coast in the British Isles, has sadly been dubbed 'slag heaps on sea'.

The dumping of colliery waste continues today, though on a smaller scale, at Nose's Point and Easington (Figs 2.37 and 2.38). Two million tonnes of solid waste a year, together with liquid slurry from collieries all over Durham, are discharged directly into the sea. The reason for this blatant pollution is simply one of cost. It is cheaper to dump the waste onto beaches and into the sea than to adopt more costly, but less environmentally damaging solutions. What British Coal is doing is perfectly legal, and there are not even laws to force the polluter to clean up the beaches which have been spoiled.

Attitudes towards the issue

Colliery waste tipping in Durham is a controversial issue because of the opposing views or attitudes held by the different parties involved. On the one hand the government and British Coal favour the continuation of tipping on the coast, and on the other, Durham County Council and Easington District Council are strongly against it. Like most environmental issues, attitudes centre around the value attached to the environment, and the costs of solving the problem. The government and British Coal believe that other methods of waste disposal would be too costly; that the price of Durham coal would increase, resulting in pit closures and job losses. The County and District Councils argue that the state of the beaches is unacceptable, and that, as the whole nation benefits from Durham coal, it is the nation that should pay for the clean-up.

Some comments on the issue of coastal pollution in Durham:

'. . . we shall not be satisfied until the tipping of colliery waste on the coast stops . . . we think that there are alternative ways of disposing of the colliery

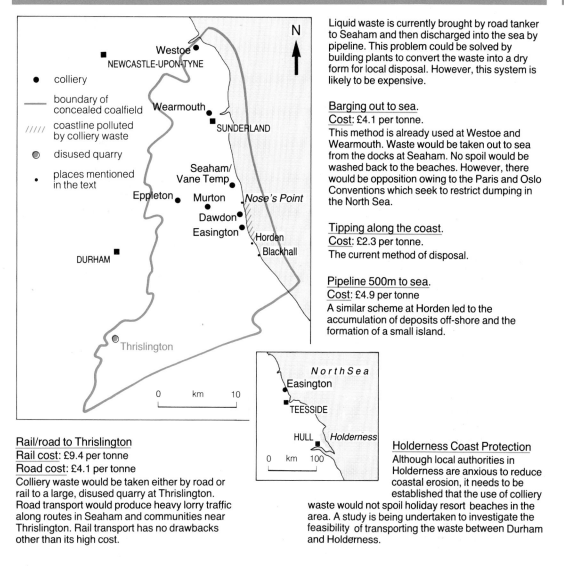

Liquid waste is currently brought by road tanker to Seaham and then discharged into the sea by pipeline. This problem could be solved by building plants to convert the waste into a dry form for local disposal. However, this system is likely to be expensive.

Barging out to sea.
Cost: £4.1 per tonne.
This method is already used at Westoe and Wearmouth. Waste would be taken out to sea from the docks at Seaham. No spoil would be washed back to the beaches. However, there would be opposition owing to the Paris and Oslo Conventions which seek to restrict dumping in the North Sea.

Tipping along the coast.
Cost: £2.3 per tonne.
The current method of disposal.

Pipeline 500m to sea.
Cost: £4.9 per tonne
A similar scheme at Horden led to the accumulation of deposits off-shore and the formation of a small island.

Rail/road to Thrislington
Rail cost: £9.4 per tonne
Road cost: £4.1 per tonne
Colliery waste would be taken either by road or rail to a large, disused quarry at Thrislington. Road transport would produce heavy lorry traffic along routes in Seaham and communities near Thrislington. Rail transport has no drawbacks other than its high cost.

Holderness Coast Protection
Although local authorities in Holderness are anxious to reduce coastal erosion, it needs to be established that the use of colliery waste would not spoil holiday resort beaches in the area. A study is being undertaken to investigate the feasibility of transporting the waste between Durham and Holderness.

Figure 2.38 The issue of colliery waste tipping in Durham: possible solutions

waste which should be paid for by the nation as a whole. The coal from Durham pits is not just burned on local house fires but is used for electricity generation – particularly in South East England.'
Local councillor (1986)

'The government is pressing us more and more to look towards tourism as a means of creating jobs and we are trying to do this. It is obvious, however, that tourists are not going to come to the despoiled parts of our beaches. We have been pressing the Minister to take steps to make our beaches into places where visitors will be pleased to come.'
Leader of Easington District Council (1986)

'We shall be telling the Minister that enough is enough. We realise that it may cost more to deal with the colliery waste in a civilised manner, but we cannot accept that the Durham coast should have to tolerate this environmental disaster. The rest of the country is getting its coal at the expense of our environment.'
Chairman of the county's environmental committee (1985)

'This is wholly unacceptable.'
Secretary of State for the Environment after seeing the polluted beaches in 1985

'The practice of tipping colliery spoil along the Durham coast has been recognised as a serious environmental problem by successive governments for over 20 years. There are, however, no easy solutions which do not pose a threat to jobs . . . the costs of transportation (to other sites) could not be borne by the collieries concerned without placing their future in jeopardy thus posing a serious threat to jobs in an area of high unemployment.'
Secretary of State for the Environment (1986)

'We have closely examined these proposals (ie alternative waste disposal solutions) and have carefully considered whether these additional costs should be funded by central government. We have concluded that this would not be in accordance with this government's commitment to the polluter pays principle. It must be for the industry – and ultimately the consumer – to pay the costs of meeting the environmental standards of the day.'
Secretary of State for the Environment (1986)

'We regard the state of the affected part of the County Durham coastline as quite unacceptable and we recommend that an early date, at least within five years, should be set by which all tipping of colliery waste on the foreshore of the UK must come to an end.'
Royal Commission on Environmental Pollution (1984)

Exercise

Complete the following exercise using the evidence of the quotes given above, the photograph (Fig 2.37), and the definition of terms in Table 2.4.

1 Describe the attitudes of those quoted towards the issue of colliery waste disposal.

2 The local councillor believes that tipping should stop for two reasons. What are they?

3 Why does the Leader of the District Council believe that the beaches should be cleaned up?

4 Explain the Secretary of State's beliefs about the issue.

5 What value is held by the Royal Commission on the issue?

6 Explain in full your own attitude, values, and beliefs towards the issue.

7 Why do you think that local people living in Easington might have mixed feelings about the issue?

Table 2.4   Investigating issues: definition of terms

Issue	A problem where individuals or groups have conflicting views.
Attitude	A person's positive or negative feelings towards an issue. For example, you may be for or against tipping on Durham's beaches.
Value	What a person *desires* to be true. For instance you may put a higher value on protecting the environment than protecting jobs.
Belief	What a person *thinks* is true. You may believe that governments will only act to protect the environment when it is in their interest to do so.

Solutions

The ultimate solution to the problem is a complete end to tipping on the coast. However, there seems little immediate prospect of the government accepting this. In fact, environmental improvements along the coast have only occurred when a pit has closed, as at Blackhall and Horden, just south of Easington (Fig. 2.38).

There are several alternatives to tipping on the coast and these have been presented by Durham County Council to the government and British Coal (Fig. 2.38). Unfortunately, they all have one thing in common: they are more expensive than the current method of waste disposal. However, there is one new proposal which could solve the problem *and* be acceptable to the government. This would involve transporting the colliery waste by barge to the Holderness coast of Humberside, where it is urgently needed to protect the soft boulder clay cliffs from rapid coastal erosion.

Oil and Gas

Oil and gas, like coal, are fossil fuels. They were formed from the remains of tiny plants and animals which lived in the sea over 50 million years ago. When they died they sank to the sea bed where they were soon buried beneath layers of sand and silt. Slowly the weight and pressure of these sediments converted the soft parts of their remains into oil and gas. Later, earth movements squeezed the oil and gas into permeable rocks, which were then folded into simple upfolds or *anticlines* (Fig. 2.40). Where there was a capping of impermeable rock, the oil and gas were trapped, ensuring their survival to the present day as a major source of energy (Fig. 2.39).

Figure 2.39 A large oil refinery at Bahrein in the Persian Gulf

Exercise

1 Using Figure 2.40 write a sentence to describe two ways in which oil is trapped.

2 In 1984 the world's total production of oil was 2826 million tonnes, the reserves were estimated at 96 000 million tonnes. Assuming that no additional reserves are discovered (which is unlikely), and that production remains constant (also unlikely), when will the world's oil reserves be exhausted?

3 How do the world's oil reserves compare with coal reserves? (Refer to page 62 for a comparison.)

World oil production and consumption

Oil accounts for two-fifths of the energy used in the world every year (Fig. 2.1). However, the pattern of production and consumption is very uneven. Between them, the USA, USSR and Saudi Arabia produce half of the world's oil. Consumption is dominated by the rich, industrialised nations of the northern hemisphere, especially in North America and Europe, and Japan (Fig. 2.41). Although they contain only one-quarter of the world's population, these countries consume three-quarters of the world's oil. Indeed, the USA alone consumes more oil than the whole of Africa, Latin America and Asia (excluding Japan) together! Because the demand for oil is so great in the industrialised countries, it can only be met by massive imports. The source of these imports is shown in Figure 2.42.

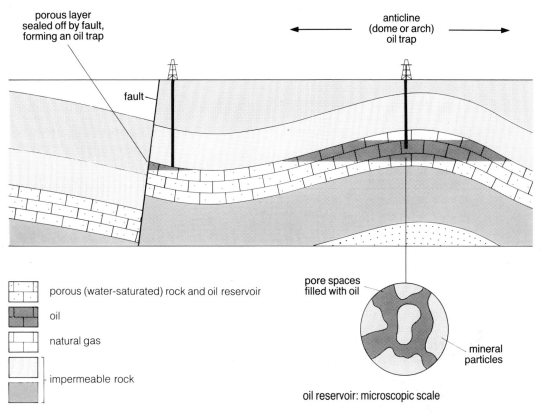

Figure 2.40 Cross-section of a typical oilfield

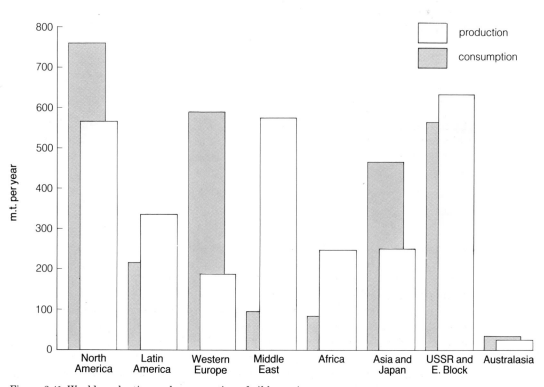

Figure 2.41 World production and consumption of oil by region

Exercise

1 Which continents/countries in Figure 2.41 consume more oil than they produce?

2 Which continents/countries/regions are likely to export oil to the industrialised countries that consume much more than they produce?

3 On which region do a) western Europe and Japan, b) the USA, rely most for their oil imports (Fig. 2.42)?

4 Use an atlas and try to explain the differences in the origin of the oil imported to western Europe and Japan, and that imported to the USA.

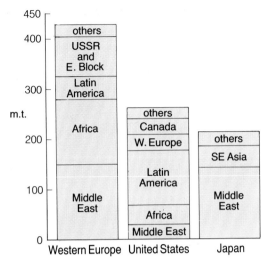

Figure 2.42 Origin of oil imports

The world's oil *reserves* are unevenly spread among the producing regions of the world (Fig. 2.43), with over half of them in the Middle East (ie the Islamic region from North Africa to Iran). This uneven distribution means that some of the largest producers of oil today – notably the USA and USSR – could run out of oil by the end of the century.

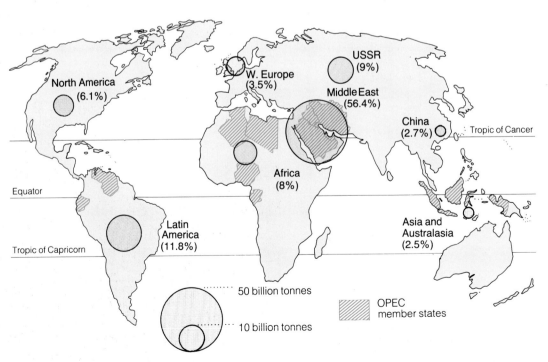

Figure 2.43 World oil reserves

Table 2.5   Oil reserves of the top ten producers

	Annual production (mt)	Reserves (mt)	Reserves:Production (R/P) ratio in years
USSR	613	8600	?
USA	494	4400	?
Saudi Arabia	230	23000	?
Mexico	150	6800	45.3
UK	126	1800	?
China	115	2600	22.6
Iran	109	6600	60.5
Venezuela	98	3700	37.8
Canada	74	1100	14.9
Indonesia	70	1200	17.1

Exercise

1 Suggest two things that countries might do to make their reserves last longer.

2 As oil reserves in the USSR and USA run out, where are these countries likely to turn for their oil supplies? (Refer to Fig. 2.43.)

3 The R/P ratio indicates how many years reserves will last. Complete the R/P ratio calculations in Table 2.5. Which country has reserves which will last longest?

4 Based wholly on the information in Table 2.5, when will reserves in the USSR and USA run out?

If you have completed the last exercise, you will know that the rich industrialised countries will, in future, have to rely increasingly on the Middle East for their oil supplies. Given the recent wars and unrest in this region, such a prospect is not an attractive one. Since 1956 there have been three wars between Israel and her Arab neighbours, a revolution in Iran, and a prolonged war between Iran and Iraq (Fig. 2.44). The war between Egypt and Syria, and Israel in 1973, led to an acute oil shortage in the West, as Arab producers cut off supplies to countries they regarded as pro-Israeli. This action prompted the first *oil shock*; a four-fold increase in oil prices which plunged the world into deep recession for the rest of the decade. A second oil shock was sparked-off in 1979 following the Iranian revolution. Once again, supplies to the West were disrupted, although this time the effects were less severe (Fig. 2.45).

Figure 2.44 The Gulf War between Iran and Iraq, 1988. The war started in 1980, and at various times has threatened oil supplies to Japan and the West

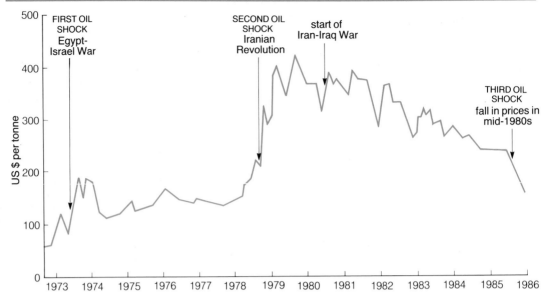

Figure 2.45 World oil prices 1973–86

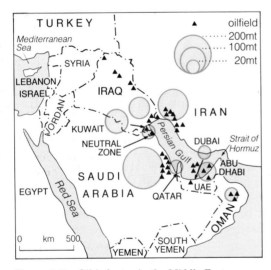

Figure 2.46a Oil industry in the Middle East

Table 2.6   Members of the Organisation of Petroleum Exporting Countries (OPEC)

Algeria	Iran	Libya	Saudi Arabia
Ecuador	Iraq	Nigeria	United Arab Emirates
Gabon	Kuwait	Qatar	Venezuela
Indonesia			

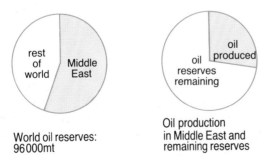

World oil reserves: 96 000mt

Oil production in Middle East and remaining reserves

Figure 2.46b Oil reserves in the Middle East

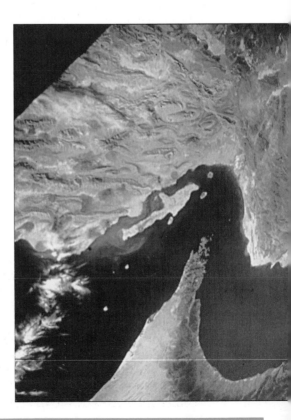

Figure 2.47 Satellite image of the Strait of Hormuz

Exercise

1 By referring to Tables 2.5 and 2.6, find out which of the world's top ten oil producers belong to OPEC.

2 Use an atlas to find out:
 a Which OPEC states are in i) the Middle East, ii) South America.
 b Which is the only OPEC state in South East Asia?

3 Suggest one reason why countries such as the USA, USSR and the UK do not belong to OPEC. (Clue: look carefully at the name, OPEC.)

4 Several oilfields in the Middle East are clustered around the Persian Gulf (Fig. 2.46a). A large proportion of the oil produced by the fields is exported by tanker through the Gulf.
 a Name the strait (Fig. 2.47) through which tankers must pass to leave the Persian Gulf.
 b How wide is this strait?
 c Can you suggest why countries such as the USA, Japan and those of western Europe should be particularly concerned about this narrow stretch of water? (Clue: which country borders the strait to the north?)

North Sea oil and gas: a diminishing resource

The North Sea is one of the richest oil and gas regions in the world. Oil and natural gas occur in sedimentary rocks, in shallow waters between 50 and 200 metres deep. In order to allow the fair development of these reserves, *median lines* (Fig. 2.48) were established which divided up the North Sea between the countries with fringing coastlines. The UK and Norway have the two largest sectors, although the Netherlands, West Germany, Denmark and Belgium each have small stakes in the North Sea. However, virtually all of the oil, and most of the gas finds, have been in the British and Norwegian sectors.

Gas was first discovered in the West Sole field in the UK sector, in 1964, and started to come ashore the following year. The first oil strike was in the Ekofisk field in the Norwegian sector (Fig. 2.48), where production began in 1971. Oil from the UK sector started flowing in 1975, from the small Argyll field. Thereafter, development was rapid, so that today, the North Sea yields around 160 million tonnes of oil a year, with 126 million tonnes coming from the UK sector.

Exercise

Study the map of North Sea oil and gas fields (Fig. 2.48) and answer the following questions:

1 How does the depth of water change from south to north in the North Sea?

2 Three of the first four British oilfields to be developed were Argyll, Auk and Montrose.

What do these fields have in common and how might this explain their early development?

3 In what way were these first oilfields similar to the early collieries in British coalfields? (Refer back to page 63 if you are not sure.)

Before 1965, almost all gas in the UK was manufactured from coal. With the discovery of North Sea gas, the gas industry switched from manufacturing to distribution. Gas was transferred by undersea pipelines to east coast terminals at Bacton, Threddlethorpe and Easington (Fig. 2.48), and then fed into the gas grid. Many oilfields also contained large reserves of gas, but until the completion of the Far North Liquids and Associated Gas System, or FLAGS (a network of pipelines for collecting gas from the northern oilfields), this gas was simply flared-off. Now the gas is piped ashore to the St Fergus gas terminal in eastern Scotland. Today, North Sea gas provides one-fifth of the UK's energy needs, and two-thirds of this comes from the UK sector. The rest is imported by pipeline from the Norwegian sector, principally from the Frigg gas field. In fact, Norway's entire production of North Sea gas is exported (look at page 25 for an explanation), with West Germany being the main customer.

Exercise

Look carefully at Figure 2.48 before answering the following questions.

1 Which oilfield is linked by pipeline to Flotta?

2 Which oilfield accounts for the bulk of the oil landed at Cruden Bay? (See paragraph on page 92.)

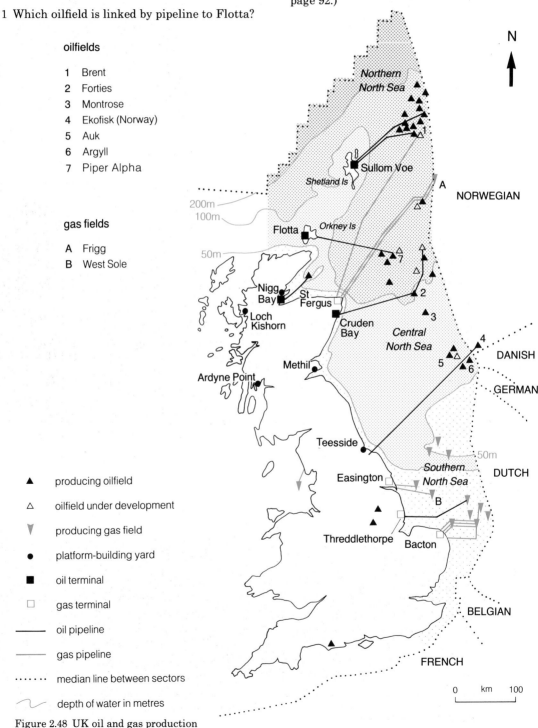

oilfields

1 Brent
2 Forties
3 Montrose
4 Ekofisk (Norway)
5 Auk
6 Argyll
7 Piper Alpha

gas fields

A Frigg
B West Sole

▲ producing oilfield
△ oilfield under development
▽ producing gas field
● platform-building yard
■ oil terminal
□ gas terminal
── oil pipeline
── gas pipeline
······ median line between sectors
〰 depth of water in metres

Figure 2.48 UK oil and gas production

3 Why is the oil terminal at Teesside not included in Table 2.7?

4 In 1986 the UK produced 129 million tonnes of oil. What proportion of this production was transferred to the UK by pipeline (see Table 2.7)? What do you think happened to the rest?

Table 2.7 Oil terminals receiving oil from the UK sector by pipeline

Terminal	Oil (mt)
Sullom Voe (Shetland) (Fig. 2.51)	56.1
Flotta (Orkneys)	15.7
Cruden Bay	24.3
Nigg Bay	2.2

Figure 2.49 The Brent C production platform in the northern North Sea. Frequent storms make the North Sea one of the most hazardous oil- and gas-producing regions in the world

Figure 2.50 Aberdeen harbour, Scotland, the main service centre for the UK's North Sea oil industry

Figure 2.51 Sullom Voe oil terminal, Shetland, which handles the largest part of the oil piped ashore from the UK's North Sea oilfields

By 1985 there were 28 oilfields and 13 gas fields in operation in the UK sector of the North Sea. However, it is likely that all of the major oilfields have now been discovered. As the chances of finding another giant, like Forties or Brent, are remote, the oil companies have turned to the smaller fields, some with reserves of less than 10 million tonnes. Meanwhile the main centre of activity is shifting northwards, into deeper water. Smaller fields and deeper water mean higher costs for the oil companies, so that increasingly the development of new oilfields depends on the price of oil. With large oilfields such as Brent, where costs are as low as US $6 per barrel, profits are guaranteed. But with smaller fields like Highlander and Deveron, costs are twice as high, and profits disappear when oil prices are low. The really small fields like Eider and Ettrick, can only be developed when prices are high – at least $20 per barrel.

Exercise

1 Draw a graph like Figure 2.52b to show production costs in oilfields A–O (Fig. 2.52a). The values for production costs are given in Table 2.8.

Table 2.8   Oilfield production costs (US $ per barrel)

Water depth (m)	Size of reserves (mt)				
	0–10	11–25	26–50	51–100	101–200
25–50	16	14	12	9	6
51–100	22	19	15	11	8
over 100	26	22	17	12	9

2 Which oilfield has a) the highest, b) the lowest production costs?

3 Give two reasons to explain the high costs in the oilfield you selected in 2a.

4 If the world price for oil were $20 a barrel, which oilfields would be unprofitable and therefore not enter production? What feature do these oilfields have in common?

5 If the world price for oil were $10 per barrel, which oilfields would be unprofitable? Say what feature these fields have in common.

6 At $10 per barrel, oilfield M comes into production, but not oilfield B. Why is this?

7 Governments may want to encourage the oil companies to develop the smaller, less profitable oilfields. This could be done by reducing the taxes that governments place on oil. If the world price for oil were $20 per barrel, what cut in taxes would be needed to make all of the oilfields in Figure 2.52a profitable?

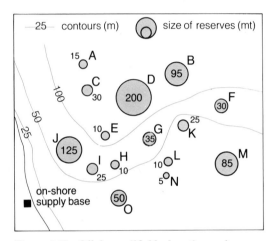

Figure 2.52a Off-shore oilfields; location and size (mt)

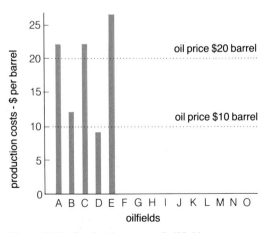

Figure 2.52b Production costs of oilfields

The future

The UK's position as a major oil and gas producer is only a temporary one. Oil and gas are non-renewable resources, and the UK's reserves are small compared to those of Saudi Arabia, Mexico, Iran and other leading producers. Even so, it is not easy to forecast accurately how long UK oil and gas reserves will last. This is due partly to the difficulty of forecasting future demand, and partly to the possibility of finding new reserves. It is also possible that new techniques for recovering more oil from *existing* fields will be developed. It may surprise you to learn that at the moment only 20–30% of the oil in any field is ever recovered. Already the oil companies are working on techniques which, if successful, will increase this proportion substantially.

However, the large oilfields in the UK sector of the North Sea have already passed their peak of production, and by the turn of the century the country's oil and gas reserves could be exhausted. Much will depend on the success of exploration in the deep waters to the west of Orkney and Shetland. Certainly the government believes that the fall in oil and gas reserves will create an *energy gap* by the mid-1990s, when the country will no longer be self-sufficient in energy (Fig. 2.53a). As we shall see later, the plan is to fill this gap by the expansion of the nuclear power industry.

Exercise

Table 2.9 shows that estimates of reserves often vary widely.

1 Figure 2.53b shows that the UK's period of self-sufficiency in oil will be short-lived. For how many years will the UK have been self-sufficient according to a) the high, b) the low forecast in Figure 2.53b?

2 If no further oil reserves are discovered in UK waters, how long will existing reserves last according to Table 2.9, given an annual production of 120 million tonnes?

Table 2.9   Estimates of North Sea oil reserves in the UK sector

Reserves remaining in present	
oilfields:	800–1950 mt
Potential future discoveries:	330–2825 mt

3 Assuming the most favourable situation in Table 2.9, and an annual production of 120 million tonnes, how long will UK reserves last?

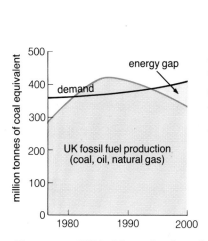

Figure 2.53a UK fuel demand and supply

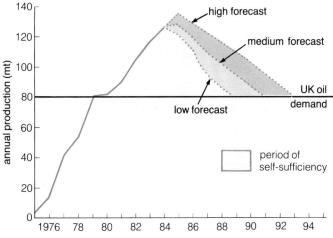

Figure 2.53b Oil production from the UK continental shelf

The oil industry and the environment

Oil pollution at sea can arise as a result of ships colliding and running aground, blow-outs and explosions on oil rigs, and fractures in underwater pipelines. These events are accidents, but the worst pollution results from *deliberate* discharges of tankers at sea, when oil tanks are washed illegally. The effects of a large-scale spillage are most damaging in coastal areas. Not only does it affect wildlife, but it may destroy the livelihoods of thousands of people employed in the fishing and tourist industries (Fig. 2.54).

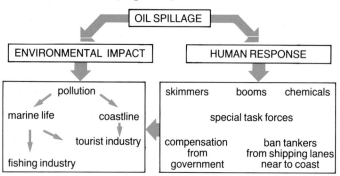

Figure 2.54 Oil pollution and its impact

The *Amoco Cadiz*: the worst ever oil disaster

The world's worst oil spillage from a tanker occurred in 1978 along the coast of Brittany in north west France, when the supertanker *Amoco Cadiz* ran aground, and spilled most of its cargo of 230 000 tonnes of crude oil. The ship was only a few kilometres offshore when its steering gear failed. Completely disabled, it was driven in heavy seas towards the coast, until it struck rocks near Portsall (Fig. 2.55), and broke in two. The result was a major environmental disaster for the coast between Le Conquet and Port Blanco (Fig. 2.56).

Enormous efforts were made to prevent the oil from reaching the shore, with booms (floating timber barriers) stretched across narrow bays and inlets, and

Figure 2.55 The *Amoco Cadiz* being broken up by heavy seas near Portsall on the Brittany coast, 25 March 1978

Figure 2.56 Oil pollution from *Amoco Cadiz* along the Brittany coast

polystyrene used to soak up the oil. However, only limited use was made of detergents to disperse the oil: in previous spillages, such as the *Torrey Canyon* disaster in Cornwall in 1967, chemical detergents had done more damage to wildlife than the oil itself. Where pollution could not be prevented, the army removed thousands of tonnes of oily sand in bags from beaches.

'The freshening wind of the Atlantic brings in the stench of oil with every gust, making the fishermen's cottages uninhabitable and fouling the grass of the farmland far inshore. Every tide brings up more oil. The rocks along the shore are jet black. The little rock pools are covered with rainbow rings of grease. The fish that are not dead are inedible and the oysters are tainted. Holiday-makers, sure that their favourite holiday beach will be covered in tar this summer, have started to cancel reservations.'
The Times, 21 March 1978

In spite of all the efforts to minimise the effects of the spillage, the extract from *The Times* shows that fishing and tourism were badly affected. The thick heavy oil settled on oyster beds and suffocated the shellfish; and commercial fish farming of salmon, trout, lobsters and crabs was also hard hit. Even two months after the accident, fishermen were being advised not to fish within eight kilometres of the coast. Three months later, at the start of the holiday season, oil still fouled many beaches, and hotels were empty. Although both fishermen and hoteliers were eventually compensated by the French government, there remained considerable anger that supertankers should be allowed to use sea lanes so near to the Brittany coast. Nonetheless, it was wildlife which suffered most from the spillage. A report by the US Environmental Protection Agency described the *Amoco Cadiz* disaster, in which 20 000 seabirds and millions of shellfish perished, as 'the worst ever for wildlife' of its kind.

Figure 2.57 Young volunteers helping to clear Brittany's beaches of oil, following the *Amoco Cadiz* disaster

The Ekofisk blow-out

Until the explosion which destroyed the Piper Alpha oil platform in 1988 (Fig. 2.59), the most serious pollution incident in the North Sea oilfields was the Ekofisk blow-out (Fig. 2.58). The blow-out occurred in 1977 when an automatic safety valve was unable to control a sudden surge of pressure in the well. Oil gushed to the surface and spilled into the sea at a rate of 3000 tonnes a day,

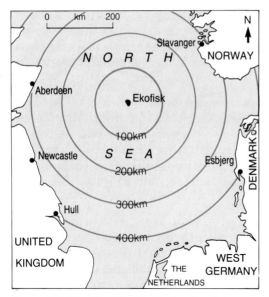

Figure 2.58 The Ekofisk oilfield, showing distances to European coasts

Figure 2.59 The remains of the Piper Alpha oil platform, wrecked by an explosion in July 1988 which killed 167 people. Oil production from Piper and its associated fields normally accounts for around 12% of the UK's North Sea output

threatening a major pollution disaster. Blow-outs are unpredictable and difficult to control, and there is always a risk of the well catching fire. A blow-out at the Wicked Witch well in the Gulf of Mexico had, for example, blazed for seven months before being extinguished. Fortunately the Ekofisk well did not catch fire, and it was eventually 'capped' at the fifth attempt by the Red Adair fire-fighting team from Texas. Altogether the blow-out lasted for eight days, spilling 24 000 tonnes of oil into the North Sea, and forming an oil slick which was 35 kilometres long, and 5 kilometres wide.

Oil pollution from the blow-out posed a serious threat to the rich North Sea fishing grounds, especially to fish that live and spawn near the surface. Despite this, the Norwegians decided against using chemicals to break up the slick. They reasoned that chemicals would cause the oil to sink to the sea bed where it would have been an even greater hazard to marine life. Instead, booms were used to prevent the slick from spreading, and a fleet of skimmer boats was used to suck up the oil. Although this was only partly successful, the slick was eventually dispersed by the action of the waves and by evaporation. Little long-term damage was done to the fishing grounds, and none of the oil reached the coast.

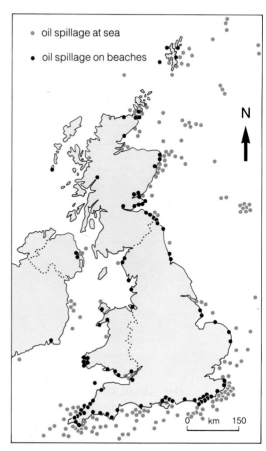

oil spillage at sea
oil spillage on beaches

Figure 2.60 Oil spillage incidents in the British Isles 1979

Exercise

1 Measure the distance from Ekofisk to the nearest stretch of coastline using Figure 2.58.

2 If the oil from the Ekofisk blow-out had not broken up, which coasts would have been polluted if the wind direction for several days had been from: a) the south west, b) the north west, c) the east?

3 Give *two* reasons why the *Amoco Cadiz* disaster had more serious environmental effects than the Ekofisk blow-out.

Exercise

Refer to Figure 1.60, which shows the distribution of oil spillages around the UK coast, and complete the following exercise.

1 Which stretch of coastline (south, east, west) has the greatest concentration of spillages?

2 Along the south coast there is a concentration of spillages in Kent and Sussex. Why is this? (Clue: look at a map of the English Channel in an atlas, and compare the shape of its western and eastern ends.)

3 What is likely to be the main source of spillages in the North Sea?

4 Can you suggest why there are relatively fewer spillages along the North Sea coast compared with the English Channel?

The greenhouse effect: changing climate and rising sea level

The global demand for energy has risen steeply in the last 200 years. As we have seen, this demand has been met largely through the burning of fossil fuels. As a by-product, huge amounts of carbon dioxide (CO_2) have been released into the atmosphere. It is no surprise, therefore, to learn that in the past 200 years, there has been a dramatic increase in the amount of CO_2 in the atmosphere. Indeed, in the short period between 1958 and 1980, CO_2 levels rose by nearly 7%. The effects of this build-up are only now being appreciated, but they are potentially very serious.

The earth's atmosphere can be compared to a greenhouse. Like the glass in a greenhouse it is transparent to the sun's rays. However, when the sun's rays strike the earth they are converted to heat, some of which is absorbed by CO_2 in the atmosphere. (In a similar way the glass in a greenhouse stops much of the heat escaping and keeps temperatures above those outside.) As long as CO_2 levels are unchanged, there is a balance between the amount of energy entering and leaving the atmosphere (Fig. 2.61), and temperatures remain constant. But with increasing levels of CO_2, more heat is being absorbed, and global temperatures slowly rise.

These small but steady increases in temperature are already leading to some melting of the polar ice caps, with the result that, worldwide, sea level has risen by some 15 centimetres since the start of the century. Most experts believe that this trend will continue, and that by the year 2100, sea level could be two or three metres higher than today. The risk of flooding in low-lying coastal areas is, therefore, a very real one. Indeed, the UK government believed the threat was serious enough to spend £800 million on the Thames flood barrier, to protect London.

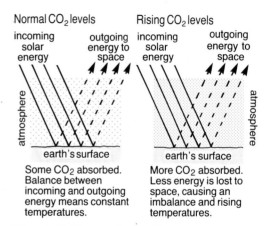

Figure 2.61 The greenhouse effect

Figure 2.62 The Antarctic ice sheet, covering some 12.6 million km and with a maximum depth of 4.3 km is the world's largest store of fresh water. The steady melting of the ice sheet is likely to raise sea level by 2 or 3 metres in the next hundred years, threatening many of the world's most densely populated areas

However, not all scientists accept the view that sea level will continue to rise slowly. It has been suggested that the melting of the great West Antarctica ice sheet is about to begin, and that within the space of your lifetime sea level could rise by as much as 15 metres! The effect of such a change in the UK would be extremely serious, but for a low-lying country like the Netherlands it would be catastrophic. All this points to the need for urgent international action to limit the burning of fossil fuels and to reduce the amount of CO_2 released into the atmosphere.

Exercise

Figure 2.63 shows the areas of Europe that would be flooded if the Antarctic and Greenland ice caps were to melt. In order to show just how serious the risk is, work through the following exercise.

1 Refer to an atlas and locate the cities listed in Table 2.10.

2 Compare the locations of these cities with Figure 2.63 and make a list of those which would be flooded by rising sea levels.

3 Again, refer to your atlas and name two countries (apart from the Netherlands) which would be completely/almost completely drowned by a rise of sea level of 65 metres.

4 In addition to providing the homes for millions of people, suggest another reason why the loss of land below 65 metres would be so serious.

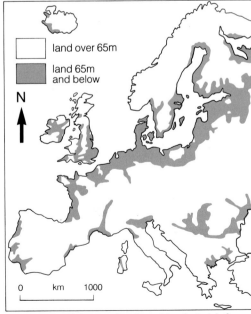

Figure 2.63 Rising sea levels and land at risk from flooding

Table 2.10 Europe's largest cities

Paris	Budapest	Copenhagen
London	Barcelona	Munich
Madrid	Hamburg	Naples
Athens	Milan	Lyons
Berlin	Warsaw	Prague
Rome	Vienna	Rotterdam
Bucharest	Stockholm	Marseille

Nuclear power

Nuclear power is produced by the splitting or *fission* of uranium atoms. This process is controlled inside a *nuclear reactor* (Fig. 2.64) and the heat that is given off is transferred by a *coolant* (which may be pressurised gas or water) to generate

a   Nuclear fission

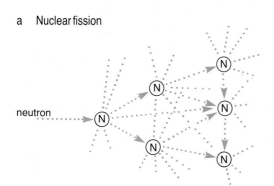

Neutrons collide with the nuclei of uranium atoms, releasing energy and further neutrons and setting up a chain reaction.

(N)   uranium nucleus of protons and neutrons

b   Nuclear power station

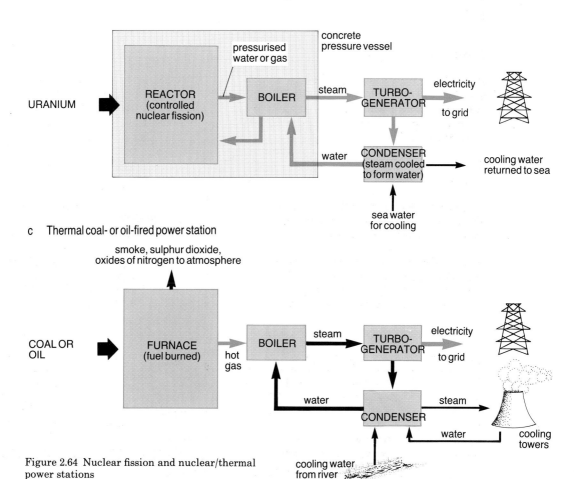

c   Thermal coal- or oil-fired power station

Figure 2.64 Nuclear fission and nuclear/thermal power stations

steam. Reactors which use a gas coolant are known as *advanced gas-cooled reactors* or AGRs; those using water are *pressurised water reactors* or PWRs.

World nuclear power production: energy for the rich

Nuclear power provides approximately 5% of the world's energy. Although this is only a small proportion, it represents a fivefold increase over the last 10 years (Figure 2.66) and further rapid expansion is expected in future. Over 95% of all nuclear power is concentrated in North America, Western Europe, Japan and the USSR. Given the amount of money and the advanced technology needed, it is not surprising that the nuclear energy industry has, as yet, made little impact in the poorer, less developed countries of the world.

Exercise

Study the four pie-charts in Figure 2.67.

1 Which countries rely on imports for more than half of their energy?

2 Which countries have the smallest fossil fuel and HEP resources *compared* to their total energy consumption?

3 In which country is a) nuclear power, b) HEP most important?

4 Look at domestic fuel production and nuclear energy production in France, Sweden and West Germany. Describe what happens to nuclear energy production as domestic fuel production decreases. How could you explain this?

Although one tonne of uranium has the energy equivalent of 1500 tonnes of oil, nuclear power is *not* an unlimited source of energy. In fact, the world's total uranium reserves are quite small, and until recently there were fears that rising demand might outstrip supplies. However, the discovery of new reserves in the 1980s has eased the situation.

Uranium reserves in the non-communist world are concentrated in Canada, the USA, Australia and South Africa (Fig. 2.68). In each of these countries there are problems facing uranium mining. Canada has been reluctant to export uranium to

Figure 2.65 The Trawsfyndd nuclear power station in Wales. As the station is located within the Snowdonia National Park, special consideration was given to blending the buildings into their surroundings

countries which use the plutonium recovered from spent uranium fuel to make nuclear weapons. In the USA there is concern about the health and safety of uranium mineworkers, exposed to hazardous radiation. Meanwhile the development of extensive reserves in Australia has been postponed for environmental reasons, and in South Africa political unrest among black mineworkers is a constant threat to uranium exports.

Uranium supplies could last well into the future if spent uranium fuel from nuclear reactors is reprocessed (see page 109). At the moment most countries store their spent fuel, but a few (including the UK and France) re-process it and use it again in nuclear reactors. Looking further ahead, the fast (or breeder) reactor, which burns plutonium, actually produces *more* fuel than it uses! If difficult technical problems can be solved, uranium could be the answer to the world's energy problems in the next century.

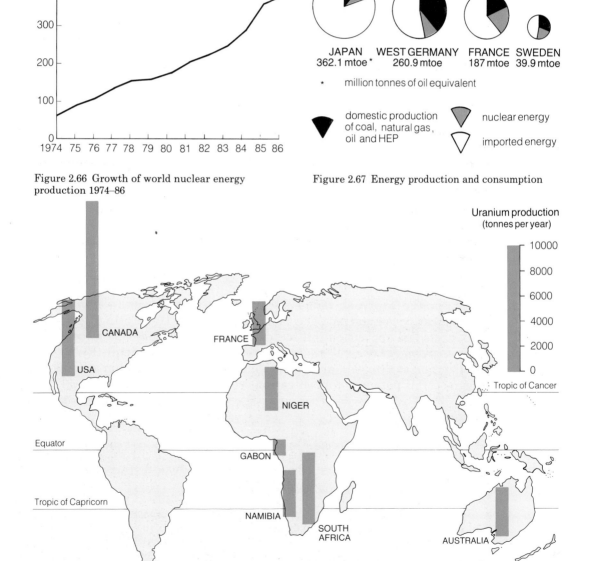

Figure 2.66 Growth of world nuclear energy production 1974–86

Figure 2.67 Energy production and consumption

Figure 2.68 World uranium production (excluding the USSR and the eastern bloc)

The UK nuclear energy industry

The world's first commercial nuclear power station was opened at Calder Hall in Cumbria in 1956. Today the UK has the world's sixth largest nuclear industry, and generates nearly 20% of its electricity from this source. Fifteen nuclear power stations were in operation in 1988 (Fig. 2.69) and a further two are planned to come on-stream by the end of the decade.

The first nuclear stations were built between 1962 and 1971. They were relatively small, ranging from 257 MW to 990 MW. They were followed by the advanced gas-cooled reactors (AGRs), which were larger and of different design. However, although the AGRs were planned in the 1960s, they have been plagued with problems. Dungeness B, for example, was started in 1966, but did not produce electricity until 1984! There have been similar delays at Hartlepool and Heysham I, and none of the AGRs have achieved an output anywhere near their design capability.

The UK government wants to expand the nuclear power industry, arguing that in the 1990s, the run-down of North Sea oil and gas will create an *energy gap* (see page 93). Rather than rely on imported oil and gas, the government would prefer to fill this gap by expanding nuclear power production. It also believes that, in the long run, electricity generated by nuclear power will be cheaper than that produced from coal, oil or gas.

The location of nuclear power stations

Two factors dominated the location of the early nuclear power stations: a) safety and b) nearness to large amounts of water for cooling. Remote locations, such as Wylfa in North Wales, and Sizewell in Suffolk, were chosen in order to minimise the risk to the public in the event of an accident. A 'remote site' was defined as one which had fewer than 600 000 people living within a 16 kilometre radius of a power station! The need for cooling water meant that all but one station was located on the coast. After 1967 the remote siting policy was relaxed: the new AGRs were thought to be incapable of any serious accident, and the emphasis shifted from the *number* of people living close to nuclear stations, to the *speed* with which they could be evacuated in an emergency.

A feature of the location of several AGRs is their siting alongside older stations, leading to the emergence of *nuclear parks*. Because of public hostility towards nuclear power (everyone wants cheap electricity but no one wants to live next door to a nuclear power station), the Central Electricity Generating Board (CEGB) encounters less opposition if it builds new power stations on existing sites, rather than on *greenfield* ones. With a new pressurised water reactor (PWR) station under construction at Sizewell, and the probability of a third station at Hinkley Point in Somerset, this policy of concentration seems set to continue.

Exercise

1 Which sites in the UK are occupied by two nuclear power stations?

2 Which is the only nuclear power station not located on the coast (Fig. 2.69)?

3 Which two power stations have the largest populations living within a 35 kilometre radius (Fig. 2.70)? Using an atlas, list some of the towns and cities located close to these power stations.

4 Coal-fired power stations also need large amounts of water but few are located on the coast. Why is this? No resources on coastal areas

5 Study Table 2.11 and describe what happens to nuclear power production in regions where there is a) no coal, b) plenty of coal.

6 In a couple of sentences explain the situation you described in your answer to question 4.

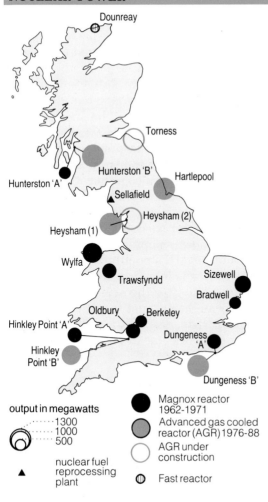

Figure 2.69 Distribution of nuclear power stations in the UK

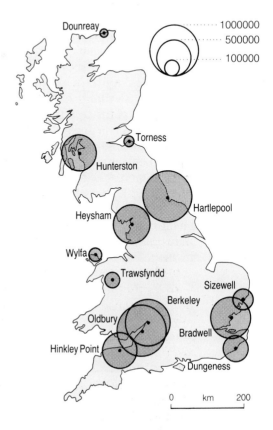

Figure 2.70 Population living within 35 kilometres of a nuclear power station in the UK

Table 2.11   Nuclear power stations and coal production by region in the UK

Region	Number of nuclear stations	Coal output (mt a year)
South West	4	0.0
East Anglia	2	0.0
South East	2	0.50
Wales	2	7.24
Scotland	2	5.28
North West	1	3.11
North	1	11.14
Yorks & Humberside	0	24.88
East Midlands	0	29.94

Nuclear power and the environment

Plutonium (a by-product of nuclear fission) is so lethal that an amount the size of a grapefruit is sufficient to kill the entire world population. Furthermore, if plutonium gets into the environment, it remains radioactive for thousands of years. Virtually all stages of the *nuclear fuel cycle* (Fig. 2.71) from the mining of uranium ore to the disposal of radioactive waste (radwaste), are surrounded by controversy and accidents involving nuclear power are of a different order to those in the coal, oil or gas industries.

Reactor safety

Except for minor leaks, there have been no serious accidents at any British nuclear power stations in nearly 30 years of operation. However, the accident in the USSR, at Chernobyl (page 105) in 1986, suddenly made the public aware of the potential dangers of nuclear power. Following Chernobyl, three-quarters of the population were opposed to any expansion of the UK's nuclear industry, and one-third wanted to see the country's nuclear power stations closed altogether. One European country – Sweden – has already decided that the risk from nuclear power is too great, and plans to phase out its four nuclear power stations by the year 2010.

Although the design of the Chernobyl reactor was quite different from British reactors, a Chernobyl-type accident in a densely populated country like the UK would be devastating. Over two-thirds of the UK's population lives within 100 kilometres of a nuclear power plant: this is less than the distance between the city of Kiev (which was partly evacuated after the accident) and Chernobyl (Fig. 2.73). Moreover, a nuclear disaster might not just result from equipment failure or human error. Sabotage by terrorists, or explosions in nearby industrial plants such as oil and chemical works (as at Hartlepool) could also lead to a nuclear disaster.

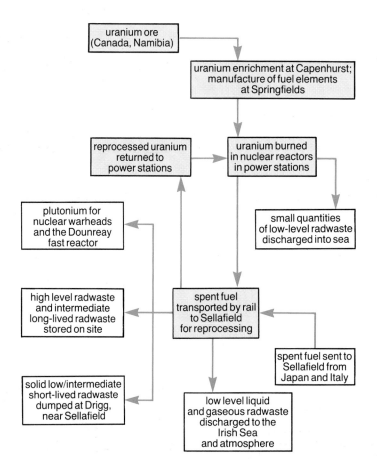

Figure 2.71 The nuclear fuel cycle in the UK

Exercise

Study the geography of reactor safety by working through the following exercise.

1 On an outline map of the UK, show the sites of the nuclear power stations (Fig. 2.69) and locate and label the following cities: London, Manchester, Liverpool, Sheffield, Leeds, Bristol, Nottingham, Newcastle, Glasgow and Edinburgh.

2 Draw circles of approximately 100 kilometres radius around each power station site (this is similar to the distance between Chernobyl and Kiev – the city from which a large part of the population was evacuated). Shade in the areas of your map which are *more* than 100 kilometres from a nuclear power plant.

3 How many of the major cities listed in (1) are within 100 kilometres of a nuclear power station? From your map, where are the safest regions in the UK in the event of a nuclear accident?

The area contaminated by a nuclear accident is determined not only by the site of the accident, but also by the direction of the wind. In this way radioactive fall-out is spread downwind, well beyond the 100 kilometre zone. Thus even the safe areas you shaded on your map of the UK could be heavily contaminated by fall-out following a nuclear accident.

Exercise

1 Given the distribution of nuclear power stations (Fig. 2.69) and the fact that the pre-vailing winds in the UK are from the south west, which of the following three counties is a) most likely, b) least likely, to be contami-nated by fall-out from a nuclear accident: Cornwall, Oxfordshire, and Fifeshire?

2 Which is the nearest nuclear power station to your school? How far away is the station? If there were a serious accident at the plant, in which direction would the wind need to blow to put you in most danger?

3 It has been said that there is no such thing as a remote site for nuclear power stations in the UK. Do you agree? Write a short para-graph on your views.

Chernobyl: the world's worst nuclear accident

On 26 April 1986 one of the two reactors at the Chernobyl nuclear power station in the Ukraine caught fire. The fire was soon out of control, and a violent explosion blew the roof off the reactor building, releasing a deadly radioactive cloud into the atmosphere.

The wind carried the cloud northwards (Fig. 2.74), and, within two days, levels of radiation in Scandinavia were reported to be one hundred times above normal.

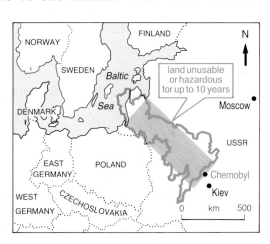

Figure 2.72 Chernobyl nuclear accident: 'The vast area that experts fear may be hazardous for a decade – almost as big as England and Scotland combined' (Source: *The Times* 2 May 1986)

Figure 2.73 Chernobyl nuclear power station after the accident of 26 April 1986

By 2 May the cloud had drifted over the UK, and on the following day heavy rain washed large amounts of radioactivity onto north Wales, northern England, parts of Scotland and Northern Ireland. Every European country was contaminated to some extent, and radioactive fall-out was even detected as far away as Japan and the USA. Eventually, ten days after the accident, the fire and radioactive releases were finally brought under control, and the reactor was entombed beneath 5000 tonnes of sand, clay and lead.

The effects of the accident were most severe in the USSR. Several workers inside the power station were killed immediately, and many others died from the effects of radiation in the weeks which followed. A few days after the accident the entire town of Chernobyl was evacuated and, in a region extending as far as Kiev (Fig. 2.73), 600 000 children were temporarily moved to safer areas.

There have also been serious economic effects. The Ukraine, known as the 'breadbasket' of the USSR, is a rich farming region, but radioactive contamination of the soil has made some areas unusable. In the worst affected areas top soil has been removed; elsewhere it could be years before radiation declines to safe levels. One expert has described an area equal in size to the distance between Brighton and Exeter in one direction, and Brighton and Aberdeen in another, where it is unsafe to raise cattle, grow fruit, vegetables and cereals such as wheat and barley. A continuing fear is that radioactivity from Chernobyl will leak into the underlying rocks and pollute the water supply of the large city of Kiev.

'The Chernobyl disaster may have sown the seeds of a deadly harvest for millions of Russians, scientists said yesterday. A huge area – as big as most of England and Scotland combined, could be hazardous for at least a decade. Many thousands of square miles of prime agricultural land could be unusable for years, forcing mass resettlement of local populations ... evacuations were likely to continue on a large scale in areas within 50 miles north of Chernobyl, and communities much further afield might be forced to abandon their collective farms and seek resettlement.

A high rate of cancer is likely within the several million people now living in that area within the next decade. "The first cases of leukaemia may start to emerge after three to five years", said Dr Mike Thomas, British Secretary of the International Commission of Radiological Protection. "A larger number of cases is likely in the following years . . . between 1,000 and 2,000 cases of cancer or inherited disease per million of the population was not unrealistic", he said.'
The Times, 2 May 1986

Exercise

Read the extract from *The Times* written shortly after the Chernobyl accident. In your own words describe the immediate, and longer term effects of the accident on the Ukraine.

Chernobyl showed that nuclear accidents are an international issue: the radio-active cloud created problems thousands of kilometres away. In northern England, upland pastures were contaminated (Fig. 2.74). Sheep and lambs grazing in the hills absorbed large amounts of radiation, making their meat unsaleable, and causing real hardship to farmers. In northern Scandinavia, where radioactive fall-out was even higher, contamination of grazing lands has been a tragedy for the reindeer-herding Lapps. Reindeer feed mainly on mosses and lichens which contain high levels of radioactivity, making their meat unfit for human consumption. Because radiation levels are likely to remain high for many years, the Lapps' traditional and ancient way of life may never recover.

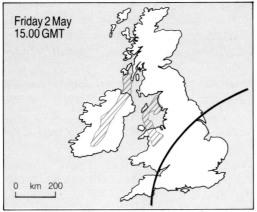

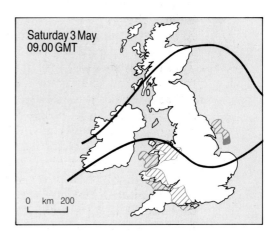

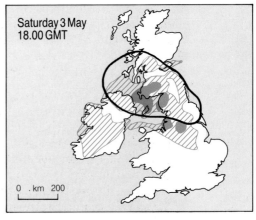

Figure 2.74 Spread of radioactivity from Chernobyl across UK. The radioactive cloud from Chernobyl reached the south east coast of Britain on 2 May, moving northwards to coincide with rain on the following day. (Source: *New Scientist*)

Figure 2.75 High levels of radiation were found in sheep and lambs on hill-farms in northern England and North Wales, following the Chernobyl accident. The animals became unsaleable, causing hardship to many farmers.

Figure 2.76 Fall-out from Chernobyl badly contaminated pastures used by the Lapps for reindeer herding in Norway and Sweden. With radiation levels likely to remain high for many years, the traditional way of life of the Lapps is threatened

Figure 2.77 Sellafield nuclear reprocessing plant, Cumbria. The photograph suggests three reasons for the location of the plant. Can you say what they are?

Nuclear waste reprocessing

Of the spent fuel recovered from nuclear reactors 96% is unburnt uranium, which if reprocessed can be used again. In the UK reprocessing is done at Sellafield on the coast of Cumbria (Fig. 2.77). Spent fuel is transported there by rail, in specially designed flasks, from the UK's nuclear power stations (Fig. 2.78). In addition,

Figure 2.78 A train carrying flasks of spent nuclear fuel from Dungeness passes through London's suburbs, heading for the Sellafield reprocessing plant in Cumbria

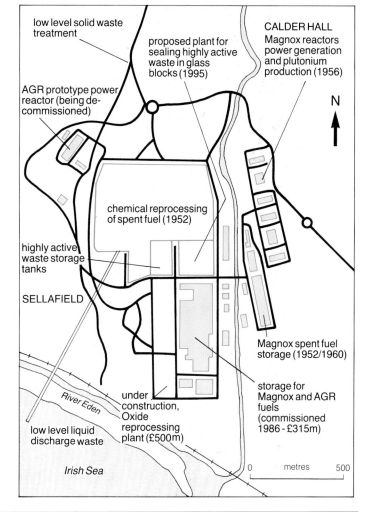

Figure 2.79 Sellafield nuclear reprocessing plant

Sellafield reprocesses spent fuel from Japan and Italy. Reprocessing is a highly profitable industry, worth hundreds of millions of pounds a year. Sellafield also employs 11 000 people, making it easily the largest employer in West Cumbria.

However, the Sellafield plant, and indeed the whole business of reprocessing, is highly controversial. This is partly because Sellafield discharges low-level radio-active waste (radwaste) into the Irish Sea (Fig. 2.79), and partly because a succession of minor accidents have allowed radwaste to leak into the environment. Some experts believe that these releases are linked to unusually high levels of cancer (particularly among children) around the plant, though this is difficult to prove. What is not in doubt is that reprocessing is potentially hazardous, and that several countries, including the USA and Sweden, prefer to store their spent fuel rather than reprocess it. In the mid-1980s discharges and leaks from Sellafield account for three-quarters of *all* radiation released to the environment in the European Community and there were calls for its closure from the European parliament and the Irish government. Since then, tighter controls have greatly reduced discharges to levels similar to those from the French reprocessing plant at Cap la Hague in Normandy.

Exercise

1 Read the two leader articles from *The Sunday Times* and *The Guardian* (Fig. 2.80) which provide contrasting views about Sellafield and reprocessing. Make a table of the main arguments of the two articles under the following headings: economic, employment, environment, and safety.

2 Make a list of any emotion-laden terms and expressions, such as 'dirty end of the business' and 'anti-nuke environmentalists' used in the articles.

3 Read the letter written by the chairman of British Nuclear Fuels Limited (BNFL) who operate the Sellafield plant (Fig. 2.81). Why in his opinion, does Sellafield get a 'raw deal'? Who does he blame for the plant's poor reputation?

4 What is your attitude towards Sellafield and the reprocessing of radwaste? Consider the economic, employment, environmental and safety arguments, and explain your attitude towards the issue in not more than 300 words.

Time to call time at Sellafield

Sellafield has now become an intolerable burden on the nuclear industry. Whether its routine discharges, of which it is the largest source in the world, or the accidental ones for which it has become notorious, are a serious environmental hazard is almost a secondary question. In the words of the Commons Environment Committee yesterday it has become a by-word for the dirty end of the business. In appraising the gap between the industry and the public, to which it devotes two chapters, the committee questions whether explanation and information can do any good. " We, as laymen, have found this inquiry technically difficult. Even understanding the basic issues and concepts has taken a considerable amount of effort." Educational exercises can make people more rather than less suspicious, and the committee quotes approvingly the evidence of a witness who said : " The very source of information, if it is in any way associated with the industry, is perceived to be fallible and possibly duplicitous." The Irish Sea is, according to the committee, " the most radioactive sea in the world ": that may still leave it perfectly safe, but try saying so to an Irish government. Fish contaminated off Sellafield turn up in Swedish waters. Harmless, maybe, but what do they do for Britain's PR ? It is the coward's way out, but Sellafield is a standing indictment the industry can never live down, at home or internationally. It will have to be closed.

Figure 2.80a Leader article from *The Guardian*, 13 March 1986

The Sellafield saga

Somebody only has to sneeze at the Sellafield nuclear waste reprocessing plant these days to get on to the front page of the nation's press. An alliance of anti-nuke environmentalists, opportunist politicians and a media establishment which cannot tell the difference between press vigilance and press vendetta seems determined to have Sellafield closed down, despite the fact that it employs 15,500 people, invests £1m a day and has won international orders worth £2.7 billion to keep it in work into the next century. Of course, nuclear safety is of crucial importance and Sellafield has to be held to account when its safety procedures are not up to scratch, and when it tries to cover up past mistakes. Last week The Sunday Times revealed one such mistake which may turn out to be far more significant than all the stories of minor leaks and non-leaks of radiation which have dominated recent headlines. This paper will continue to subject Sellafield to the utmost scrutiny. But its safety record must be seen in perspective. As far as we know, nobody has died because of Sellafield. Yet every year during this decade about 40 people have died in coal, oil and gas, with barely a footnote in the newspapers or television. Much urgent research remains to be done, of course, on the possibility of any link between radiation leaks at Sellafield and the incidence of forms of cancer in the surrounding area. But even if such a link is ever established it again has to be seen in perspective. All the evidence suggests that, even on the very worst assumptions, nuclear power is far less dangerous to your health than most other types of mass-produced energy. Since it is an international industry that Britain happens to be rather good at, we should not be in such a rush to destroy it.

Figure 2.80b Leader article from *The Sunday Times*, 23 February 1986

When Sellafield gets a raw deal from all and sundry

Sir, — It was flattering to be one of your "Friday People" (February 7), and I was grateful that you catalogued some of the past occasions on which I had become exasperated with the attitude of the media. I have not changed my mind about any of them.

However, the treatment meted out to us over the past two weeks by both media and politicians surpasses anything in the past in its blind, unreasoned, near-hysterical, reaction to two genuinely minor events.

Two weeks ago, by senior-level decision, we discharged to sea 440 kgs of purified uranium. The radioactivity involved was very low: the Irish Sea already contains many thousands of tonnes of naturally occurring uranium which is being continuously added to by rivers and miscellaneous industrial discharges. We broke no regulation and required no special authorisation; the event should have had no significance publicly.

But for us: headline treatment, demands from regulatory authorities for "explanations" and threats of prosecution if they were not satisfactory, while politicians at home and abroad demanded closure of the plant and an end to such "disgraceful behaviour."

Last week we had an incident in our reprocessing plant. Radioactivity was detected in a building. It was established that the leak was from a pump used for sampling plutonium nitrate solution, and it was corrected. During this period it was decided as a prudent measure to put the key members of site staff on to "amber alert," which merely gives notice that there may be a developing situation involving the site.

In the event matters were quickly brought under control and the "amber alert" was withdrawn. All the necessary steps were taken in case a more serious situation developed, including notifying appropriate authorities and people, and preparing an authoritative public statement.

But we were beaten to the post by the media, which clearly had received a tip-off from an unnamed source that led them to believe there was a major emergency. Wild, inflammatory, scaremongering statements were made throughout the media; we were bombarded by press, radio and TV, demanding information, comment, interviews.

Orson Welles all over again!

As is now well-known, the incident was minor; there was no risk to the public; and none of our employees was significantly contaminated. Out of 71 examined, two showed results at the "limits of detection" which *may* mean they are very slightly but not dangerously contaminated.

We in BNFL clearly have something to learn in trying to speed up still more our response time to the media and authorities in events like these, but it should be recognised that to do so under persistent pressure and with the fear that one wrong or misinterpretable statement will itself bring criticism, does not make things easy for plant managers or public information personnel.

I believe we have very competent and conscientious management and employees at all levels in the company. To talk of the safety record at Sellafield as poor, and to refer to hundreds of incidents, is nonsense.

I am not being complacent. Quite the reverse. I am deeply concerned that our employees be allowed to concentrate on the essential issues of safety and environmental protection. We have responsibilities, including those to the media and politicians; but so have they to us. — Yours faithfully,
Con Allday,
British Nuclear Fuels plc,
Risley, Cheshire.

Figure 2.81 Letter to *The Guardian* from the then Chairman of British Nuclear Fuels Ltd, 15 February 1986

The storage and disposal of radwaste

All types of industry produce waste, and the nuclear industry is no exception. However, the deadly nature of radwaste means that it needs very careful storage and handling compared to spoil from a coal mine, or ash from a power station.

Radwaste occurs as a liquid, a solid and a gas. Normally, low-level liquid and gaseous radwastes are discharged into the sea and atmosphere. In the UK, low-level solid radwaste, such as contaminated paper, equipment and clothing, is dumped in shallow trenches at Drigg, near Sellafield. Soon this site will be full, and the Nuclear Industry Waste Executive (NIREX) is searching for a new site. Such a site must be leak-proof and well away from large centres of population. Clay is the best material for storing the waste in, being not only impermeable, but also plastic, and therefore self-sealing in the event of an earthquake. Possible areas and sites for nuclear dumping are shown in Figure 2.83. The four named sites were recently investigated by NIREX and were found suitable, but strong opposition from local residents, farmers and conservationists forced NIREX to abandon its plans. Clearly radwaste has to be stored somewhere, but no one wants a nuclear waste dump on their doorstep if they can possibly avoid it.

Exercise

Read the extract from *The Guardian* (Fig. 2.82) which describes the dumping of low-level radwaste as 'amateur and haphazard'.

1 Explain why the UK's approach to the disposal of radwaste is regarded as unsatisfactory.

2 How does France dispose of its low-level radwaste?

Dumping of waste 'amateurish and haphazard'

BRITAIN'S approach to nuclear waste disposal is condemned in yesterday's report from the committee as amateurish, haphazard and complacent.

The MPs contrast the "shoe string" approach which leads to waste being dumped in a trench at Drigg, beside the Sellafield reprocessing plant, Cumbria, or stacked in a hangar at Harwell, with the scientific and carefully researched programmes they found on visits to France, Germany, Sweden and the United States.

At Drigg, supposedly used for dumping only "low-level" waste, rain water is allowed to run through earth trenches into the river Irt and from there into the Irish Sea. The waste is not packaged or labelled and some material that would otherwise fall outside the low-level radioactive category is buried there on the principle that it will be dispersed and diluted over a long period if it escapes.

This "haphazard approach to what goes into Drigg does not inspire confidence," say the MPs. It contrasts, for instance, with the careful sorting and labelling of what goes into the concrete, clay-lined trenches of the equivalent French dump at Centre de la Manche, near Cherbourg.

The MPs recommend that the waste should be compacted, sorted and labelled, with the more dangerous, longer-lived forms of radioactivity specifically excluded. The Cumbrian dump is not a satisfactory model for other sites, they say, and the nuclear industry's waste executive, Nirex, would probably agree.

Figure 2.82 Extract from *The Guardian*, 13 March 1986

The most dangerous radwaste is stored on site at Sellafield in concrete, stainless-steel-lined containers. This high-level radwaste poses a long term problem as it will remain radioactive for thousands of years. However, the total amount, though increasing every year, is small, and its disposal is not an urgent problem. For the time being it is stored as a liquid, but the plan for the future is to convert it to a glass, making it easier and safer to store and handle. Ultimately it is planned to store all the UK's high-level radwaste deep underground. possibly in tunnels excavated in granite in remote areas, such as the Scottish Highlands or Dartmoor.

Figure 2.83 Possible UK storage sites for low-level radwaste

Alternative sources of energy

The energy resources that we have looked at in this chapter have all been *non-renewable*. This means that sooner or later they will be exhausted. Indeed in the case of oil, serious shortages might begin to appear before the end of this century. This alarming prospect has prompted an interest in *alternative energy* sources which are *renewable*. At the moment, renewable energy resources make only a tiny contribution to the world's energy production.

In the UK, the alternative energy sources with the greatest potential are wind, tidal and wave power. As islands situated in high latitudes, the UK has a windy climate, as the severe gales of October 1987 made only too clear. Wind speeds are greatest near the coast, and tend to increase from south to north (Fig. 2.84). Already the Central Electricity Generating Board (CEGB) has several experimental windmills in operation and in some countries, notably Denmark, windmill parks are becoming a common sight along the coast (Fig. 2.85). In theory wind power could supply all of the UK's electricity. There is, however, one problem: 15 000 windmills would be needed, each with blades of 90 metres diameter!

The principle of tidal power is to build a barrage across an estuary, and generate electricity using differences in water level on either side of the barrage, caused by the tides. Suitable estuaries, like the Rance in northern France (Fig. 2.88) which has Europe's only tidal power station, have a large tidal range (normally more than 5 metres), a narrow mouth to reduce the costs of building the barrage, and a large storage area behind the barrage to give maximum potential power. Ten sites

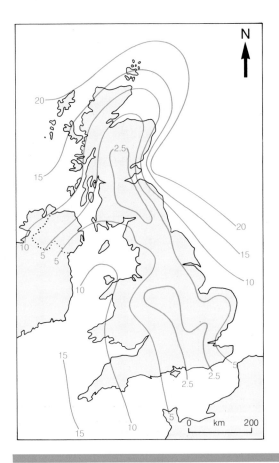

Figure 2.84 Total annual wind energy in the UK (in GJm^2). (After Mustoe)

Figure 2.85 Windmill park at Oddesund, in western Denmark. The park occupies a flat site, on an exposed, windy stretch of the North Sea coast

in the UK meet these requirements (Figs 2.86 and 2.87) including the Severn Estuary, which is the best in Europe. If all of these sites were developed they could provide around one-quarter of the UK's electricity. There are, however, some drawbacks: the initial costs of building are very high, and wildlife (especially birds and migrating fish) in estuarine areas could be badly affected, provoking the opposition of conservationists.

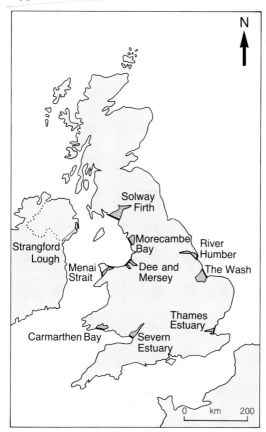

Figure 2.86 Tidal power sites in the UK

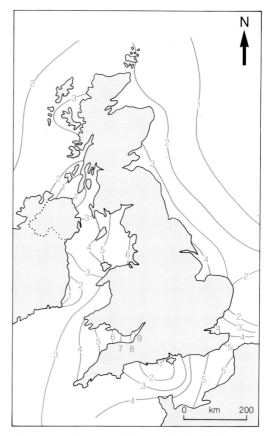

Figure 2.87 Average tidal range in the UK (in metres) (After Mustoe)

The energy present in ocean waves is enormous. Long stretches of the UK's west coast are exposed to powerful Atlantic breakers, whose energy could be harnessed by wave machines (Fig. 2.89). But here too there are obstacles to producing really large amounts of energy. Not least is the 1400 kilometre line of wave machines which would be needed to generate all of the nation's electricity using this method!

In the short term there seems little likelihood of alternative energy sources having a dramatic impact on the UK's energy position. Nonetheless, as North Sea oil and gas run out, we can expect alternative energy to make a small, but growing contribution to the country's energy needs.

Figure 2.88 The Rance tidal power station in Brittany, France

Exercise

1 Explain how alternative energy sources in the UK are all related to the fact that the country is an island.

2 Look at the maps of tidal power sites (Fig. 2.86) and average tidal range (Fig. 2.87). Describe the advantages of the Severn Estuary over other tidal power sites.

3 Differences in wave power are related to *fetch* as well as wind speed. Fetch is the distance of open water over which the wind blows. Using an atlas, find the longest fetch at the following places in Figure 2.89: Newquay, Blackpool, Iona, Aberdeen and Dover. Compare your measurements with those for wave power in Figure 2.89, and write a brief paragraph on your findings.

4 Look at Figure 2.84 and an atlas which shows the distribution of population in the UK. What is likely to be the main obstacle to the production of large amounts of electricity in the windiest areas of the UK?

Figure 2.89 Average wave power in the UK (in kW per metre) (After Mustoe)

Energy in less developed countries

The example of India

The amount of energy consumed per person in India is less than one-twentieth of that in the UK. One reason for this is that in India, as in most other less developed countries, a large proportion of the energy used is free. This *non-commercial energy* includes firewood, gathered from forests and woodland; dung from cattle; and the power of draught animals such as buffalo and oxen. Hundreds of millions of people in the less developed world depend on such energy, which, because it is free, goes unrecorded in the official figures.

Exercise

1 Calculate the amount of electricity consumed per person per year in India and the UK.

2 Suggest two reasons why the consumption of energy per person is so low in India.

Table 2.12   Energy production and consumption in India and the UK

	India	UK
Total population (m)	777	56
Electricity production (MW)	42180	66431
GNP per person/year ($)	233	6514
% workforce in agriculture	29	2
% workforce in industry	13	42
% urban population	24	92

The energy crisis in the countryside

The so-called *biomass fuels* of firewood, animal dung and farm wastes, account for 40% of India's total energy consumption. Although a massive programme of rural electrification has brought electricity to two out of three of India's 500 000 villages (Fig. 2.90), only about 8% of rural homes are connected directly to the electricity grid. The main use of electricity is to power pump-sets which supply water for irrigating farmland.

Among the rural poor, firewood is the most important fuel, especially for cooking (Fig. 2.91). Yet although forests cover nearly one-quarter of India, there is an acute shortage of firewood in many areas. Destruction of forest and woodland cover may lead

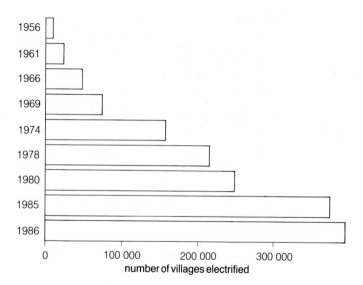

Figure 2.90 Progress of rural electrification in India

Figure 2.91 Collecting firewood in Tamil Nadu, India. Wood is the main source of fuel in the less developed world, and collecting it is mainly women's work

to soil erosion. A shortage of firewood means that the people are forced to burn animal dung, which could otherwise be used as fertiliser to increase food production.

Exercise

1 Study Figure 2.92 and find (a) the annual demand for firewood (b) the amount of new timber grown annually (c) the annual short-fall between supply and demand.

2 Explain briefly the likely impact of such a shortfall on India's forests and woodlands.

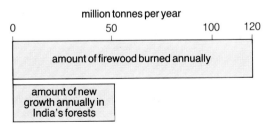

Figure 2.92 Supply and demand for firewood in India

The problem of energy shortage in rural areas can only be solved through the expansion of the non-commercial sector. One solution, which is already working, is the production of biogas. Biogas is made by placing farm waste, manure and vegetation in sealed concrete and steel containers. Heat from the sun helps bacteria to decompose these wastes rapidly, and in the process, to give off methane gas. The methane is stored and is used for cooking and lighting, either for individual households or for whole communities. Moreover, the residue from the sealed containers can be put on the land and used as fertiliser. The government is eager to promote village schemes in the poorest parts of rural India: in 1985–86 alone, 193 000 such schemes were successfully established.

The greatest demand for energy in rural areas is for cooking. However, the tradi-tional stove – the chullah – which burns firewood, agricultural wastes or cow dung, is extremely inefficient. At the moment 120 million tonnes of firewood are consumed annually for cooking, but it is hoped that the introduction of an improved chullah will eventually save up to 17 million tonnes of firewood a year.

There are an estimated 80 million cattle in India (buffalos and oxen) providing draught power for agriculture and transport in the countryside. Current research into improved designs of agricultural implements, water lifting devices and carts should make the use of animal power more efficient, making further savings of energy possible.

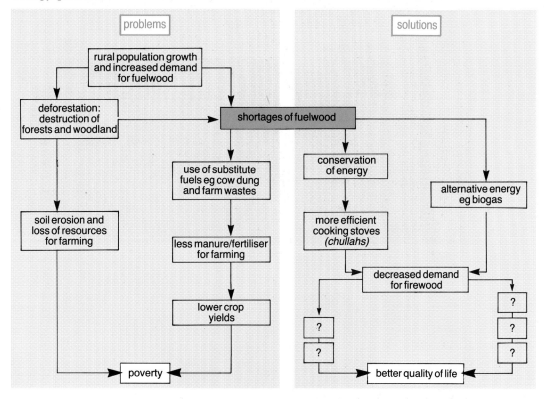

Figure 2.93 Fuelwood resources in India: problems and solutions

Exercise

Use Figure 2.93 to complete the following exercises.

1 Make a copy of Figure 2.93 in your exercise book. Study carefully that part of the diagram which describes energy problems, and then fill-in the boxes which are blank in the section covering solutions.

2 What is the main way of conserving fuel and thus reducing the destruction of forests and woodlands?

3 Why should the use of animal dung as a fuel be discouraged?

4 Apart from the need for firewood, can you think of other reasons for the destruction of forests in the less developed world?

Energy for an emerging industrial nation

Although most people in rural India depend on non-commercial energy, coal, oil, natural gas, HEP and nuclear provide the power for India's manufacturing industries, transport systems, and cities.

India's economic development is based on five-year plans, which set targets for industry and agriculture. These targets depend heavily on the expansion of commercial energy. For example, in the first plan (1955–60) a number of major river-valley projects (Fig. 2.95), involving the building of dams and the generation of HEP, were developed. The Damodar Valley project was typical: it covered an area of nearly 25 000 km², and was centred on four HEP stations and three coal-fired power stations.

Figure 2.94a A large thermal power station at Trombay, near Bombay in India. The power station generates electricity for nearby steel and engineering industries

Figure 2.94b India's atomic development centre near Bombay. Although India's nuclear industry has been developed partly for military purposes, the production of electricity from nuclear energy is important to India's plans for industrialisation

In addition to supplying cheap energy to industries like steel and heavy engineering, the construction of dams allowed floods on the Damodar River to be controlled, irrigation to be extended, and food production to be increased. So Damodar was truly a multi-purpose development project, similar to Sri Lanka's Mahaweli scheme that we looked at on pages 29–32.

Coal is the main source of commercial energy (Fig. 2.96) and India is now the world's fifth largest producer. HEP is also important (Fig. 2.96) though so far only 20% of the country's potential (mainly in the mountains of the north) has been tapped. Oil and gas production on the other hand, are modest and supply barely half of the country's needs: two-thirds of India's oil production comes from the Bombay High offshore field (Fig. 2.95). In contrast, there are huge reserves of thorium, a fuel similar to uranium which can be used in nuclear reactors. Partly for this reason India is one of the few less developed countries which has its own nuclear power industry. Currently there are five reactors in operation (Fig. 2.95), which contribute around 3% of India's electricity, and there are plans for a ten-fold expansion by the end of the century.

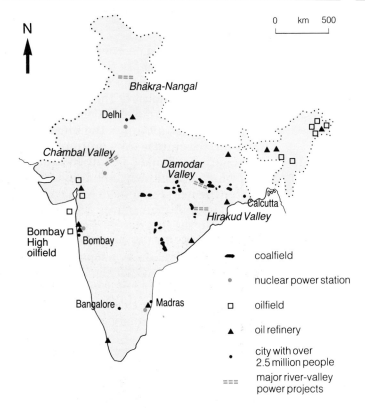

Figure 2.95 Commercial energy sources in India

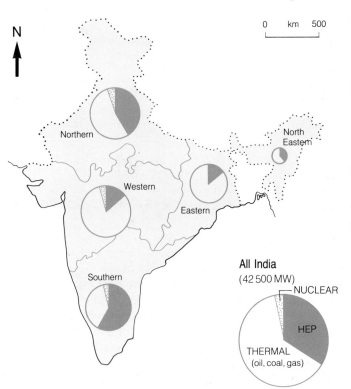

Exercise

Study Figures 2.95 and 2.96 and answer the following questions.

1 Which region in India: (a) produces the most HEP (b) is most dependent on thermal electricity (c) has a pattern of electricity production which is most similar to that for the whole of India?

2 The eastern region is heavily dependent on thermal electricity. What is the likely reason for this?

3 Look closely at the location of nuclear power stations compared to the distribution of coalfields and major cities. Suggest a possible explanation for the location of these power stations.

Figure 2.96 Electricity production in India

Summary

All societies depend on energy, whether it is electricity-generated in a nuclear power station, or simply the power of an ox-drawn plough. Generally, the more advanced the technology of a society, the greater the amount of energy consumed per person. Thus most of the world's energy is consumed by the developed countries of North America and Europe, and Japan. Most of this energy is derived from fossil fuels, although the importance of nuclear power is growing rapidly. However, fossil fuels take millions of years to form, and at current rates of consumption, oil and gas will be exhausted by the middle of the next century. Even coal, which is still plentiful, could be nearing exhaustion in 200 years' time. Sooner or later the world will have to turn to renewable sources of energy such as wind, wave, tidal and solar power. Meanwhile we should not forget that today, millions of people in the less developed countries face acute shortages of energy, particularly fuelwood, for basic needs such as cooking and heating.

The production and consumption of energy raises a number of important environmental issues. At the global scale, the 'greenhouse' effect, caused by the burning of fossil fuels, threatens at least some melting of the polar ice caps. Acid rain is an issue of worldwide concern, and its effect on soils, forests and wildlife in some countries is already catastrophic. Meanwhile at a continental scale, accidents at nuclear power stations and routine discharges of radwaste not only damage the environment, but directly threaten human health and well-being. Finally, at a local scale, landscapes are spoilt by mining subsidence, tipping and open-cast workings, and in the less developed countries forests are destroyed to supply the growing demand for fuelwood. Although planners have had some success in solving such local problems, there is little sign yet of the international effort which is needed to tackle the most urgent problems at the global scale.

Further exercises

A

Study Figure 2.97 which shows the distribution of oil- and coal-fired power stations in England and Wales.

1 What do you notice about the distribution of oil-fired power stations? Mention two points.

2 How many oil-fired power stations are located a) north, b) south of a line from the Wash to the Bristol Channel? How would you explain this distribution? (Clue: look back to Fig. 2.8.)

3 Coal-fired power stations are mainly located close to their source of fuel. Explain the reason for this location, rather than a location near the main centre of electricity demand in South East England.

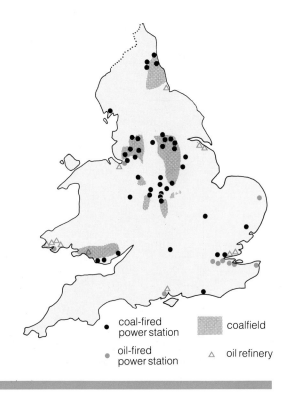

Figure 2.97 Distribution of coal- and oil-fired power stations in the UK

- coal-fired power station
- oil-fired power station
- coalfield
- △ oil refinery

B

Figure 2.98 shows an imaginary region with seven possible locations for a 1200MW power station. Six factors affect the choice of location.

- For nuclear, oil- and coal-fired power stations there must be extensive flat sites.

- All three types of power station need access to water for cooling. Cooling water is available from either the sea or rivers. If water is available from rivers there must be an average flow of at least 3 cubic metres per second (cumecs). Where cooling water is taken from rivers, supplies are limited, and expensive cooling towers must be built. There is no such restriction on water supplies from the sea, and coastal stations do not need cooling towers.

- For a nuclear power station, remoteness from large centres of population, and a location downwind of these centres is preferred.

- Transport costs for fuel are insignificant for nuclear power stations. For both oil- and coal-fired stations transport costs are high, and there are advantages in locating close to fuel supplies. Oil is available on the coast, transferred by tankers and pipe-lines from offshore oilfields. Coal is available from collieries on the coalfield.

- Air pollution from oil- and coal-fired power stations is a problem, and a location downwind from centres of population is preferred.

- All power stations try to avoid sensitive conservation areas such as estuaries, which provide important habitats and feeding grounds for wildfowl and wading birds.

- Draw three tables similar to Table 2.13 in your exercise book, one for each type of power station, ie oil-fired, coal-fired and nuclear.

Table 2.13   Site analysis: nuclear

	1	2	3	4	5	6	7
Water for cooling							
Remoteness							
Site area							
Availability of fuel	X	X	X	X	X	X	X
Downwind of city							
Conservation area							

(Words in **bold** are essential siting factors)

1 Assess the suitability of the seven sites in relation to each of the locational factors. If the site is favourable for a particular factor then insert a 1 in the table; if it is unfavourable then insert 0. For example, if a site for a coal-fired power station is on the coalfield, then fuel is available and the site would score 1 on this factor. On the other hand, if this site is upwind of a major city, then pollution might occur, and this factor would score 0.

2 Complete all three tables, and find the best site for each type of power station. Describe briefly the advantages of the three sites you have chosen.

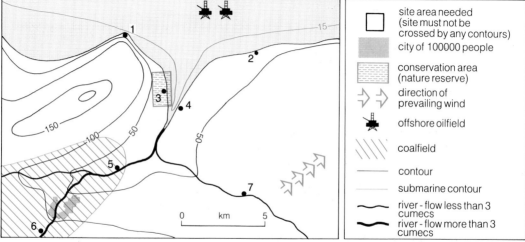

Figure 2.98 Siting a power station

Table 2.14   Decision-making exercise: building a 1200MW power station

	Arguments for nuclear power	Arguments against nuclear power
ECONOMY AND EMPLOYMENT	Over 25 years, electricity from nuclear power is cheaper: 2.45p per unit compared to 2.63p for coal.	The short term costs of energy from nuclear power are greater owing to the huge capital costs of nuclear power stations.
	British industry must have cheap energy to remain competitive.	Existing nuclear power stations have been disappointing. They have taken up to 20 years to build and have never worked at more than 70% capacity.
	The project will create about 500 permanent jobs when complete.	A nuclear power station will reduce demand for UK coal by 2mt a year and result in the loss of 2500 jobs in the mining industry.
		Pit closure has severe social as well as economic effects on mining communities.
	Nuclear power is the only option if the UK is to remain self-sufficient in energy when North Sea oil and gas run out in 10 to 15 years.	UK has huge reserves of coal, sufficient to last 300 years at current production rates.
		Energy prices fluctuate: uranium prices may rise in future relative to coal.
	Investment in nuclear power is needed to maintain UK's 'know-how' in nuclear technology. This could be a valuable export earner in future.	
SAFETY AND ENVIRONMENT	There has been no major accident at a commercial power station in the UK since the start of the nuclear power programme in the early 1950s.	A serious nuclear accident at a nuclear plant in the UK would have devastating consequences for a small, overcrowded island.
	According to the CEGB the risk of a nuclear accident is very small: an accident resulting in tens of deaths should only happen once in every 100 000 reactor years; an accident causing 100 early deaths once in 10 000 000 reactor years.	Soviet scientists claimed that the risk of a major accident like Chernobyl was equally small; American scientists made similar claims before the accident at Three Mile Island.
	UK reactors are different in design from Chernobyl.	In the USA some scientists forecast a 1:5 risk of a similar accident to Chernobyl before 2000 AD.
	Deaths in the coal industry greatly exceed those in the nuclear power industry.	It only requires one Chernobyl-type accident in the UK to make a large part of the country uninhabitable.
	Nuclear power stations are less damaging to the environment: – coal mining creates subsidence. – loss of farmland and visual amenity through tipping of colliery spoil. – 1200MW coal-fired station would produce one million tonnes of fly ash a year which would be tipped in the vicinity. – burning of coal in power stations is regarded by most scientists as the principal cause of acid rain. – greenhouse effect caused by burning of coal.	Nuclear power stations are vulnerable to terrorist attack.
		Deaths in the coal industry only affect coal miners. Accidents at nuclear power stations affect the surrounding population and are of a different order of magnitude.
		No solution has yet been found to the storage of radwaste. High-level radwaste poses particular problems.
		Reprocessing spent nuclear fuel is the major source of radiation leaking into the environment.

Table 2.14 Decision-making exercise: building a 1200MW power station

	Arguments for nuclear power	Arguments against nuclear power
SAFETY		Radiation-linked cancer among workers in the nuclear power industry: the industry pays compensation but does not admit liability. Land reclamation and restoration after mining has improved greatly: tips can be restored to farmland and subsidence controlled.
POLITICS	Electricians' union is more moderate than mine workers'. UK should seek to diversify its energy sources and not rely on a single fuel: remember the coal strike 1984/85.	Nuclear power is unpopular with the electorate. There are 'no votes in nukes!'

C

The CEGB wants to build a new nuclear power station. However, there is strong opposition from those who would prefer a coal-fired plant, and to settle the issue a public enquiry is held. The main arguments are summarised in Table 2.14. More detailed information is given in the sections on coal and nuclear energy in this chapter.

1 Select one of the following participants in the enquiry:
   – the chairman of the CEGB
   – the chairman of British Nuclear Fuels Limited (BNFL) (responsible for reprocessing radwaste)
   – the president of the National Union of Mineworkers (NUM)
   – a representative of Greenpeace or Friends of the Earth
   – a member of the public living within 5 kilometres of the site

2 Prepare an argument for *one* of the participants. Define carefully your attitude towards the issue, and in your arguments emphasise your values and beliefs (for a detailed explanation of attitudes, values and beliefs, turn to page 36).

3 Your teacher will then chair the debate, and you may be called on to explain your views to the rest of the class.

4 When the debate is completed, write a report as the inspector in charge of the enquiry, making your recommendations, and describing in detail the reasons for your decision.

D

Figure 2.99, in the colour section, is a 1:50 000 extract of part of the Yorkshire coalfield.

1 Draw a sketch map of the area at half scale, and locate the following clearly on your map: coal mines, mining spoil, the rivers Aire and Calder, marshy areas and standing water where mining subsidence has probably occurred, power stations, and the towns of Castleford and Pontefract.

2 Where are the main areas of subsidence on your sketch map? Can you suggest why subsidence has led to flooding in these areas?

3 How is coal likely to be transported from the mines. Give the evidence provided by the OS map.

4 From the evidence of the map, give two reasons for the location of the power station in 4724.

5 Using map evidence, state three possible disadvantages that coal mining and electricity generation might cause to residents in the area.

Checklist of what you should know about energy sources

Key ideas	Examples
Energy consists of renewable and non-renewable resources.	Renewable resources are inexhaustible, eg wind, wave, tidal, solar and hydroelectric power. Non-renewable energy includes fossil fuels which are being rapidly depleted.
Most of the world's energy comes from burning fossil fuels.	Oil, coal and natural gas are the leading sources of energy.
The distribution of energy resources at a world scale is highly uneven.	Oil reserves are unevenly distributed and are dominated by the Middle East. Coal reserves are more widespread. Uranium reserves are confined to just five or six countries.
The uneven distribution of oil results in important trade patterns.	The major trade in oil is between the Middle East, and western Europe and Japan.
The amount of energy consumed per person in a country depends on that country's level of technology and economic development.	Energy consumption per person is low in the less developed world, especially in Africa and Asia. High levels of energy consumption are found in North America, Europe, Australasia and Japan.
Many LDCs see the expansion of commercial energy production as a vital step towards economic development.	Industrial development in India is based on the expansion of coal, oil, gas, HEP and nuclear industries.
A large proportion of the energy consumed in LDCs is non-commercial energy.	Rural populations in LDCs depend heavily on fuelwood, animal dung, animal power and agricultural wastes. This energy, unlike coal, oil, gas and electricity is usually free, and therefore non-commercial.
The development of energy resources depends on several factors.	(1) Economic – the cost of production, eg depth, thickness, quality of coal seams; quality of uranium ore; depth of water in offshore oil and gas fields. The cost of transport, eg remoteness/accessibility of resources. World prices, ie the higher the price, the more likely that development will occur. (2) Political – eg the decision of the UK government to expand nuclear energy; the policy of the US government not to rely too much on Arab oil and to develop its own reserves; the level of taxes imposed by governments on oil and gas companies. (3) Technology – the technology to extract oil and gas reserves from offshore fields; the development of nuclear technology; mining of coal using automated methods. (4) Environmental – opposition to new developments because of the adverse effects on the environment, eg disposal of low-level radwaste, North East Leicestershire coalfield.
The production and consumption of energy often has adverse effects on the environment.	Acid rain and the greenhouse effect; spoil heaps and subsidence from mining; oil spillages and their effects on the coast; disposal of radwaste and nuclear accidents; the consumption of fuelwood in LDCs leading to forest destruction and soil erosion.

Key ideas	Examples
Planners try to minimise the impact of energy industries on the environment at a local scale.	Strict planning controls in greenfield coalfields like Selby; land restoration and reclamation in mining areas; remote siting of nuclear power stations.
The production and consumption of energy raises a number of issues.	(1) Economic – depletion of oil reserves and the choice of fuel to fill the energy gap. (2) Safety – how safe is nuclear power? Should spent nuclear fuel be reprocessed? How should radwaste be disposed of? (3) Social – should unprofitable coal mines be closed, or should they be subsidised to preserve jobs and mining communities? (4) Environmental – should the development of energy resources be halted where there is a significant threat to the environment, eg North East Leicestershire? The greenhouse effect and the problem of acid rain.

Part Three

Resources for recreation and leisure

Although most of our lives are spent doing essential things, like eating, washing, sleeping, and of course working, more and more time is spent in *recreation* and *leisure* (Fig. 3.1). These activities, which occupy much of our spare time, are done purely for pleasure. They are extremely varied, ranging from playing sport and dancing, to sunbathing and watching television. However, in this chapter we shall concentrate mainly on outdoor recreation, its provision and the pressure it places on the environment.

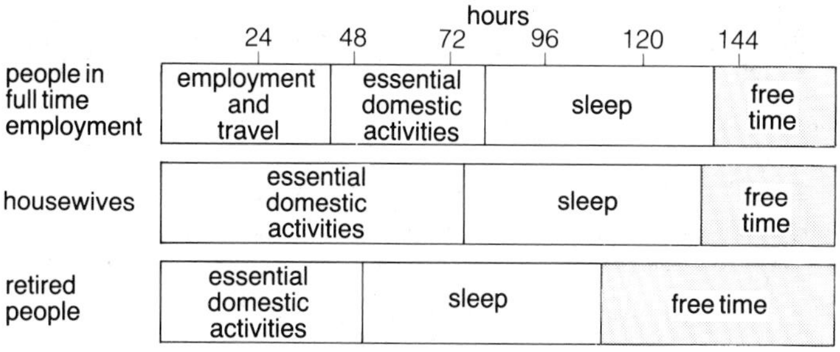

Figure 3.1 Use of time in a typical week

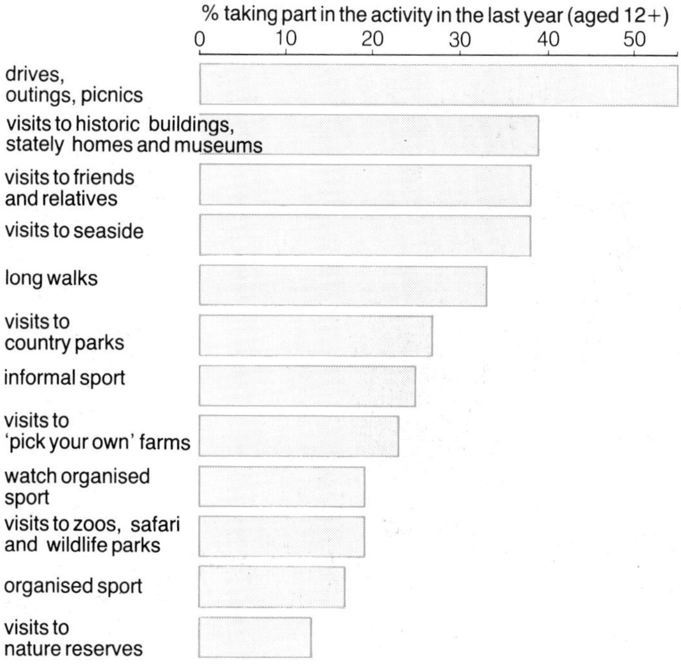

Figure 3.2 The countryside and recreational activities: England and Wales 1985

(a)

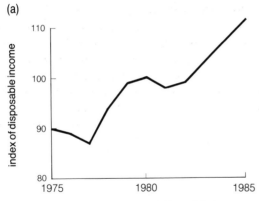

Figure 3.3a Real household and disposible incomes in the UK, 1975–85 (1980 = 100)

(b)

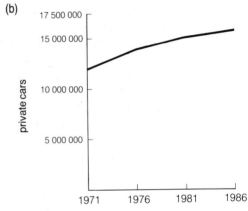

Figure 3.3b Number of private cars in the UK 1971–86

Exercise

Figure 3.2 shows the popularity of various recreational activities in England and Wales.

1 Collect similar information on the recreational activities of the members of your class during the last year, and present the information as a bar graph. Add extra categories to your graph for any other activities not covered by Figures 3.1 and 3.2.

2 Describe the main differences between your graph and Figure 3.2. Try to explain these differences. (Clue: opportunities for recreation in your local area, differences in recreational preferences between teenagers and adults.)

(c)

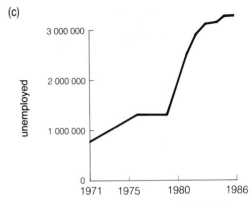

Figure 3.3c Numbers of unemployed in the UK 1971–86

In all developed countries there has been a huge increase in the demand for recreation in recent years. There are several reasons for this:

- A reduction in working hours and an increase in holiday entitlement has meant that people have more spare time.
- Rising living standards have given people more money to spend on recreation (Fig. 3.3a).
- A rapid growth in car ownership (Fig. 3.3b) has greatly improved access to the countryside, the coast and other recreational attractions. Meanwhile, the cost of air travel has fallen, boosting foreign holiday travel.
- Earlier retirement at 55 and 60 for many workers, made possible by job pension schemes, has increased the demand for recreation among older people.
- Rising levels of unemployment since the 1970s (Fig. 3.3c) have forced millions of people, especially the young, to have more spare time, some of which is spent on recreation.

Our spare time is not spread evenly throughout the day or week or year. Spare time comes in 'blocks', such as weekends and summer holidays, and how we spend it depends on the size of the block. Recreation outside the home usually involves travel, and generally, the more spare time we have the more time we are prepared to spend travelling. For instance, with four or five hours to spare on a Sunday, we might be prepared to visit a local beauty-spot within an hour's drive. We call such a visit a *day* or *half-day trip*. However, with a two-week holiday, we might easily spend a day or more travelling to our destination. We use the term *tourism* to describe this type of recreation which involves overnight stays away from home.

Exercise

1 Keep a diary of how you spend your time during a typical school week, from Monday to Friday. Record in hours how much time you spent sleeping, working (school day, homework, household duties, and travel to school), eating, on personal care, and on leisure activities (watching TV, watching and playing sport, visiting friends and relatives etc.). Present this information as a pie-chart.

2 Keep a similar diary for a weekend and present this information as a pie-chart too. Then: a) compare the two graphs and describe the main differences, b) try to explain these differences.

Conservation, recreation and leisure

National parks are quite different from the *urban parks* of towns and cities. One obvious difference is that whereas urban parks are usually no larger than a few football pitches, national parks cover hundreds of square kilometres (Fig. 3.4). Furthermore, while urban parks are used exclusively for recreation, national

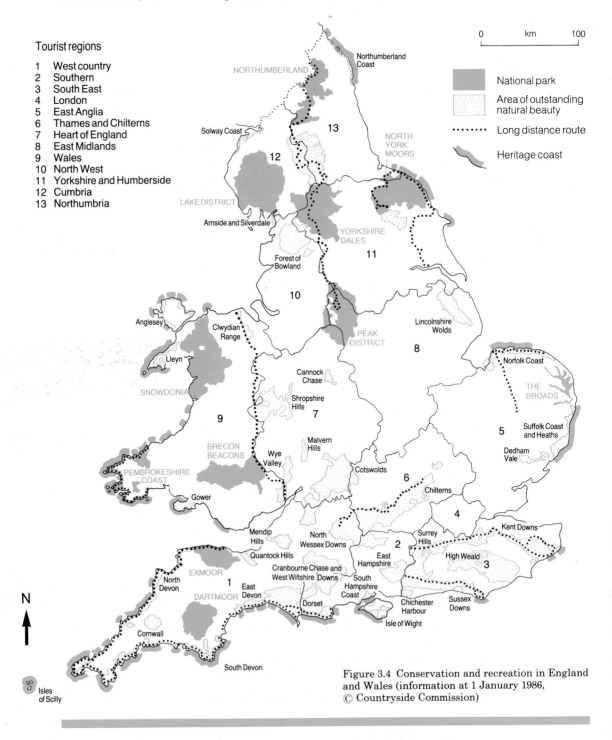

Tourist regions

1   West country
2   Southern
3   South East
4   London
5   East Anglia
6   Thames and Chilterns
7   Heart of England
8   East Midlands
9   Wales
10   North West
11   Yorkshire and Humberside
12   Cumbria
13   Northumbria

Figure 3.4 Conservation and recreation in England and Wales (information at 1 January 1986, © Countryside Commission)

parks are used for farming, water catchment, military training, forestry and quarrying, as well as recreation (Fig. 3.5). Finally, unlike urban parks, which are owned by the public authorities, most land in national parks belongs to private individuals.

The ten national parks were set up between 1951 and 1957 (Table 3.1); all of them occupy areas of great natural beauty. Except for Pembrokeshire, they are mainly rugged upland areas dominated by moorland (Fig. 3.6). They are managed by specially appointed National Park Committees (NPCs) whose main tasks are to control new building and development, and provide information services and limited facilities for visitors. In this way the NPCs aim both to protect the landscapes and wildlife of the parks *and* promote their use and enjoyment by the public.

Exercise

Study Figures 3.4–3.7 then complete the following exercises:

1 Which national parks are situated *wholly* to the north and west of the Tees–Exe line, in the so-called Highland Zone of Britain? In a single sentence describe the distribution of national parks in England and Wales.

2 Match the lists of national parks and upland areas given below:

Lake District	Pennines
Peak District	Cheviot Hills
Yorkshire Dales	Cumbrian Mountains
Northumberland	Pennines

3 Which national park is: a) the largest, b) the smallest, c) the one with the most farmland?

4 The NPCs encourage 'quiet' recreational activities which neither damage the countryside nor disturb other people. Which of the following recreational activities would you say are likely to be a) encouraged, b) discouraged in national parks?:

Water-skiing, fishing, hang-gliding, powerboat racing, canoeing, bird-watching, motor-scrambling, walking, rock-climbing and pony-trekking.

Table 3.1　Milestones in the creation of national parks

1944　The Dower Report recommended the setting up of national parks.

1949　National Parks and Access to the Countryside Act. The Act defined national parks as 'extensive tracts of country of great natural beauty which afford opportunities for open air recreation'. The Act set out the aims of national parks – to preserve their natural beauty and promote their enjoyment by the public.

1951　Designation of the Lake District, Peak District, Snowdonia and Dartmoor national parks.

1952　Designation of the North York Moors and Pembrokeshire Coast national parks.

1954　Designation of the Yorkshire Dales and Exmoor national parks.

1956　Designation of the Northumberland national park.

1957　Designation of the Brecon Beacons national park.

1968　Countryside Act. Although conservation and recreation remained the main aims of national parks, planners had also to take account of the needs of agriculture, forestry and employment for people living in the parks. Conservation of the *landscape* was made the responsibility of the Countryside Commission; conservation of *wildlife* became the responsibility of the Nature Conservancy Council.

1974　The Sandford Report established the principle that when there was a conflict between conservation and recreation, conservation should be given priority.

1986　Designation of the Norfolk Broads as a conservation area on similar lines to a national park.

The national parks are not all equally popular: while the Lake District attracts over 20 million visitors per year, Northumberland barely receives one million (Fig. 3.7). Such unevenness in popularity results in part from differences in the number of people living within easy travelling distance of each park (Fig. 3.8). The great majority of visitors are day-trippers who normally come from within a radius of 90 minutes travelling time by car. If the journey takes much longer, then a day trip is often ruled out, and people will visit an alternative attraction.

Exercise

Test the idea that the larger the number of people living within easy travelling distance of a national park the greater its popularity, by working through this exercise.

1 Complete Table 3.2 using the information given in Figure 3.8. For city size category 100 000–199 999 use an average population of 150 000; for category 200 000–299 999 use 250 000; for cities of more than 300 000, use the actual populations given in Table 3.2

2 Compare the popularity of the Peak District and Pembrokeshire as shown by your calculations, with the actual numbers of visitors given in Figure 3.7. Do the numbers of people living close to national parks appear to affect their popularity? Comment in a few sentences.

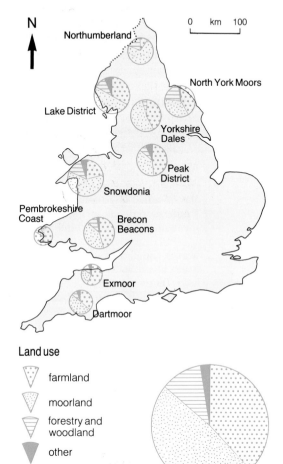

Figure 3.5 Land use in the national parks

Table 3.2 Population in towns of more than 100 000 within 100 kilometres of each national park

Northumberland	687 000
Lake District	869 000
North York Moors	1 685 000
Yorkshire Dales	3 658 000
Peak District	?
Snowdonia	874 000
Brecon Beacons	2 904 000
Pembrokeshire Coast	?
Exmoor	1 295 000
Dartmoor	360 000

The last exercise should have demonstrated that differences in the popularity of national parks does not just result from the number of people who live close by. No account, for instance, was taken of the *accessibility* of each park. Parks such as the Lake District and Peak District are well served by the motorway network, and are much easier to get to than Snowdonia or Northumberland. Sometimes, even though a park is close to a large centre of population, it may receive fewer visitors than expected. This can happen when another park, offering similar attractions, is even closer, and acts as an *intervening opportunity*. For example, parts of the Yorkshire Dales national park are within 90 minutes travelling time of Manchester. However, with the Peak District national park on Manchester's doorstep, it is vastly more popular with day-trippers from that city than the Dales. In this situation the Peak District is an intervening opportunity between the Dales and Manchester.

Finally, although all of the national parks are renowned for their beauty, some are undeniably more beautiful than others, and this increases their popularity. The spectacular landscapes of the Lake District make it the best known and most popular of the national parks, and attract an unusual number of long-stay visitors from all over the country. Other parks, such as the Brecon Beacons and Northumberland have a less obvious appeal, and inevitably attract fewer and more local visitors.

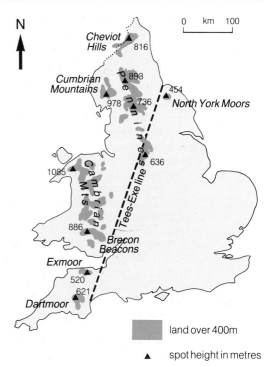

Figure 3.6 Distribution of uplands in England and Wales

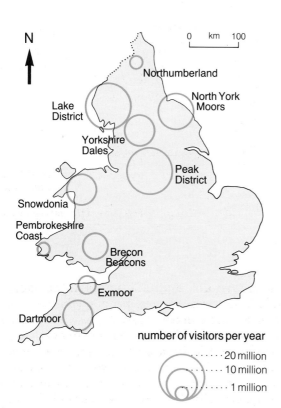

Figure 3.7 Number of visitors to national parks

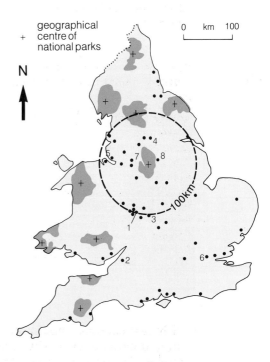

Cities of more than 300 000 people in England and Wales

1 Birmingham	100 700	5 Liverpool	510 000
2 Bristol	388 000	6 London	6 767 000
3 Coventry	314 000	7 Manchester	449 000
4 Leeds	449 000	8 Sheffield	447 000

Figure 3.8 National parks and the distribution of population in England and Wales

Exercise

1 Name the four factors which account for differences in popularity of the national parks.

2 Write a brief explanation of the influence of each factor on the number of visitors.

3 Look at Figure 3.8 and name the parks which act as intervening opportunities (assuming all parks are equally attractive) between:
   Sheffield and the Yorkshire Dales
   Plymouth and Exmoor
   Hull and the Peak District
   Cardiff and the Pembrokeshire Coast
   Newcastle-upon-Tyne and the North
      York Moors

Figure 3.9a A busy car park at Castleton in the Peak District national park. The Peak District is one of the most visited national parks, and overcrowding and traffic congestion occur at the most popular locations at holiday times and summer weekends. Most visitors are day-trippers from nearby Manchester and Sheffield.

Figure 3.9b Victim of its own popularity. Penyghent, one of the highest peaks in the Yorkshire Dales national park, receives over 120 000 visitors a year. The result is severe erosion, especially where the heavily used Pennine Way long-distance footpath crosses areas of poorly drained peat. Currently, £500 000 is being spent to try to tackle the erosion problem on Penyghent and the neighbouring peaks of Ingleborough and Whernside.

The Yorkshire Dales National Park

The Yorkshire Dales (Figs 3.10 and 3.12) is the third largest national park and is roughly the size of Surrey or Warwickshire. It became a national park in 1954, primarily to protect its unique limestone scenery (Fig. 3.11). However, in addition to its limestone features, the Dales has large tracts of wild moorland, beautiful valleys, and a wide range of recreational attractions (Fig. 3.14).

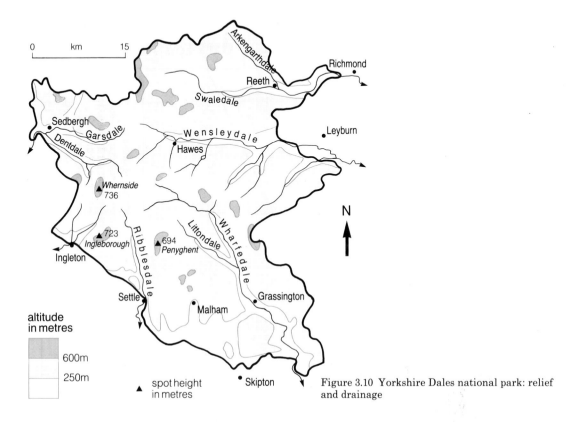

Figure 3.10 Yorkshire Dales national park: relief and drainage

Exercise

Study the 1:25 000 OS extract (Fig. 3.13b in the colour section) of part of the Yorkshire Dales and then complete the following exercise.

1 Draw a cross-section of the relief between the summit of Ingleborough (742746) and Rantree Moss (714768), using a vertical scale of 1 cm to 100 metres.

2 Using the block diagram in Figure 3.11 shade in the four major rock types on your section.

You can determine the extent of the limestone on the OS map by an absence of surface streams, and features such as dry valleys, pavements and pot holes. The summit of Ingleborough has a thin capping of Millstone Grit.

3 Add the following details to your section, using arrowed labels: limestone pavements, Raven Scar, Twisleton Scar, River Doe, Ingleborough, Rantree Moss, cave, and shake holes.

5 Identify the scar at D. What is its approximate height above sea level?

6 Name one piece of evidence from the photograph which suggests that the rock at D is different from C.

7 What type of woodland is found at E?

8 Large parts of the area covered by the photograph are used for farming:
   a) What is the main crop?
   b) Where is the best farmland situated?
   c) Using evidence from the photograph, give three reasons for your answer to (b).

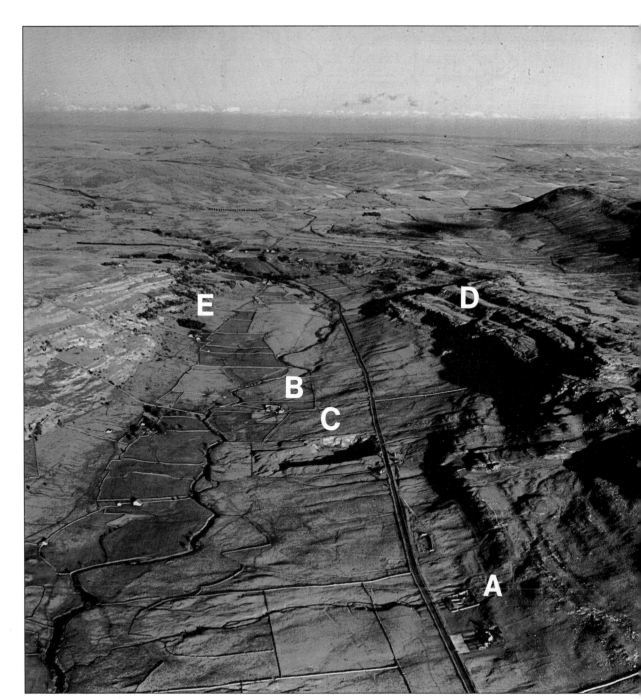

Figure 3.13a The Doe Valley near Ingleton in the Yorkshire Dales

The Yorkshire Dales National Park

The Yorkshire Dales (Figs 3.10 and 3.12) is the third largest national park and is roughly the size of Surrey or Warwickshire. It became a national park in 1954, primarily to protect its unique limestone scenery (Fig. 3.11). However, in addition to its limestone features, the Dales has large tracts of wild moorland, beautiful valleys, and a wide range of recreational attractions (Fig. 3.14).

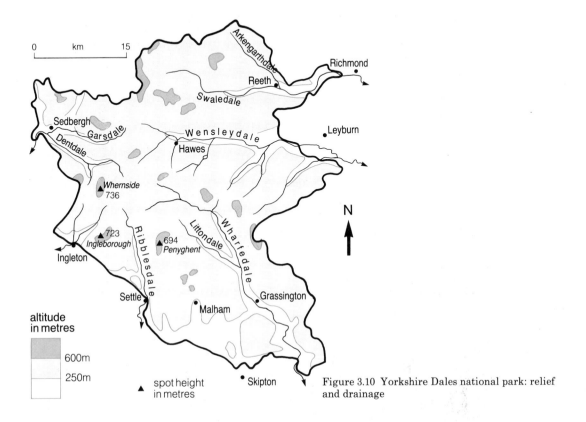

Figure 3.10 Yorkshire Dales national park: relief and drainage

Exercise

Study the 1:25 000 OS extract (Fig. 3.13b in the colour section) of part of the Yorkshire Dales and then complete the following exercise.

1 Draw a cross-section of the relief between the summit of Ingleborough (742746) and Rantree Moss (714768), using a vertical scale of 1 cm to 100 metres.

2 Using the block diagram in Figure 3.11 shade in the four major rock types on your section.

You can determine the extent of the limestone on the OS map by an absence of surface streams, and features such as dry valleys, pavements and pot holes. The summit of Ingleborough has a thin capping of Millstone Grit.

3 Add the following details to your section, using arrowed labels: limestone pavements, Raven Scar, Twisleton Scar, River Doe, Ingleborough, Rantree Moss, cave, and shake holes.

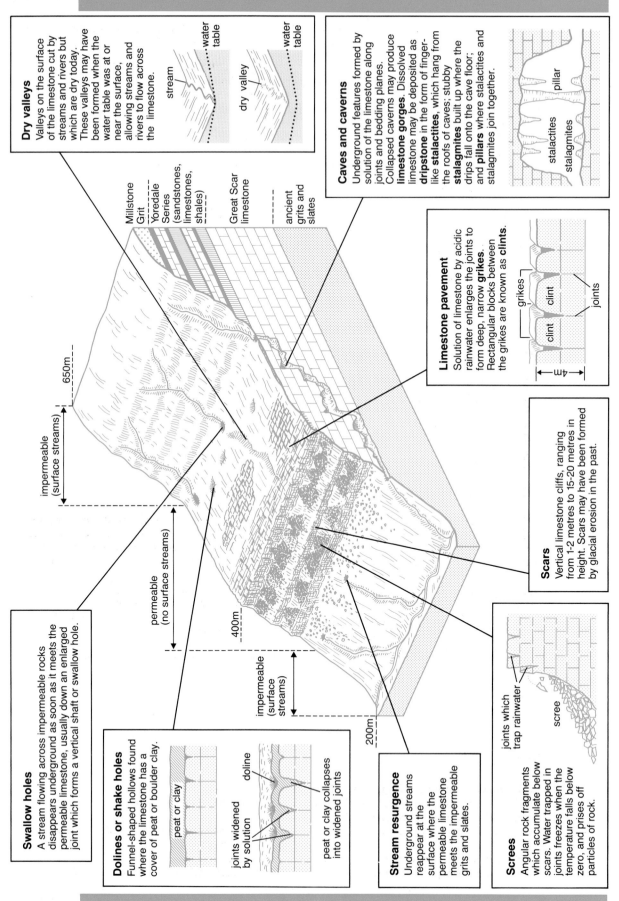

Dry valleys

Valleys on the surface of the limestone cut by streams and rivers but which are dry today. These valleys may have been formed when the water table was at or near the surface, allowing streams and rivers to flow across the limestone.

Caves and caverns

Underground features formed by solution of the limestone along joints and bedding planes. Collapsed caverns may produce **limestone gorges**. Dissolved limestone may be deposited as **dripstone** in the form of finger-like **stalactites**, which hang from the roofs of caves; stubby **stalagmites** built up where the drips fall onto the cave floor; and **pillars** where stalactites and stalagmites join together.

Limestone pavement

Solution of limestone by acidic rainwater enlarges the joints to form deep, narrow **grikes**. Rectangular blocks between the grikes are known as **clints**.

Swallow holes

A stream flowing across impermeable rocks disappears underground as soon as it meets the permeable limestone, usually down an enlarged joint which forms a vertical shaft or swallow hole.

Dolines or shake holes

Funnel-shaped hollows found where the limestone has a cover of peat or boulder clay.

Stream resurgence

Underground streams reappear at the surface where the permeable limestone meets the impermeable grits and slates.

Scars

Vertical limestone cliffs, ranging from 1-2 metres to 15-20 metres in height. Scars may have been formed by glacial erosion in the past.

Screes

Angular rock fragments which accumulate below scars. Water trapped in joints freezes when the temperature falls below zero, and prises off particles of rock.

Millstone Grit

Yoredale Series (sandstones, limestones, shales)

Great Scar limestone

ancient grits and slates

650m

impermeable (surface streams)

permeable (no surface streams)

400m

impermeable (surface streams)

200m

water table

stream

dry valley

water table

stalactites

pillar

stalagmites

grikes

clint

clint

joints

4m

joints which trap rainwater

scree

peat or clay

doline

joints widened by solution

peat or clay collapses into widened joints

Figure 3.11 Limestone scenery in the Yorkshire Dales

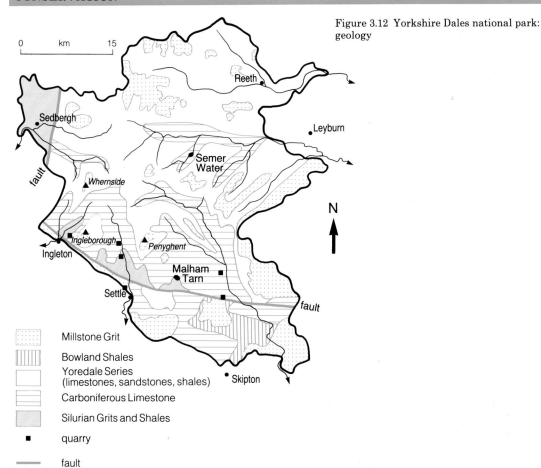

Figure 3.12 Yorkshire Dales national park: geology

Legend:
- Millstone Grit
- Bowland Shales
- Yoredale Series (limestones, sandstones, shales)
- Carboniferous Limestone
- Silurian Grits and Shales
- ■ quarry
- — fault

4 Make a list of six different features on the map extract which suggest that the area is important for tourism. Give the six figure grid reference of each feature in your list.

5 Apart from recreation and tourism, name two activities shown on the map which are found in the national park. Are these activities likely to come into conflict with recreation and conservation?

6 Imagine that you are planning a day trip to the area shown on the map, and that you can spend three hours walking and looking at some of the sights. Plan a route for your walk which must:
a) not exceed 10 km in length,
b) start and finish in the same place,
c) use only public rights of way and other footpaths.

7 Explain why you chose your route.

Exercise

Study the air photograph (Fig. 3.13a) of the Doe Valley, near Ingleton, and the OS map extract (Fig. 3.13b in the colour section), and complete the following exercise.

1 In which direction was the camera pointing when the photograph was taken?

2 Name the tourist attraction at A.

3 Name the settlement at B and give its six figure grid reference.

4 What kind of rock was quarried at C?

5 Identify the scar at D. What is its approximate height above sea level?

6 Name one piece of evidence from the photograph which suggests that the rock at D is different from C.

7 What type of woodland is found at E?

8 Large parts of the area covered by the photograph are used for farming:
   a) What is the main crop?
   b) Where is the best farmland situated?
   c) Using evidence from the photograph, give three reasons for your answer to (b).

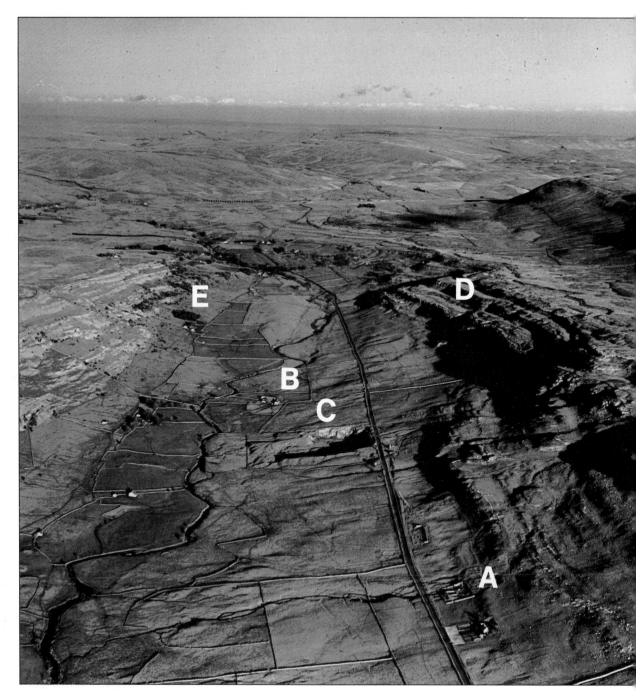

Figure 3.13a The Doe Valley near Ingleton in the Yorkshire Dales

In common with other national parks, the landscape of the Yorkshire Dales is under pressure from several activities which require large amounts of space (Fig. 3.14). Activities such as quarrying and water supply threaten the destruction of the landscape, and give rise to land use *issues*. An important task of the National Park Committees is to resolve such issues and find a balance between the protection of the countryside and local and national interests.

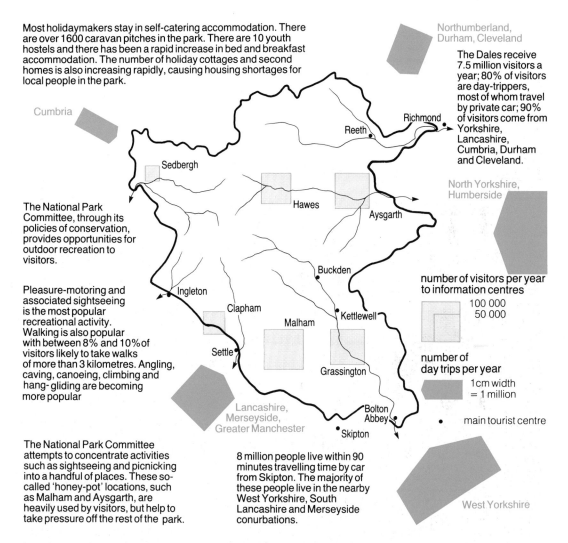

Most holidaymakers stay in self-catering accommodation. There are over 1600 caravan pitches in the park. There are 10 youth hostels and there has been a rapid increase in bed and breakfast accommodation. The number of holiday cottages and second homes is also increasing rapidly, causing housing shortages for local people in the park.

Northumberland, Durham, Cleveland

The Dales receive 7.5 million visitors a year; 80% of visitors are day-trippers, most of whom travel by private car; 90% of visitors come from Yorkshire, Lancashire, Cumbria, Durham and Cleveland.

North Yorkshire, Humberside

Cumbria

The National Park Committee, through its policies of conservation, provides opportunities for outdoor recreation to visitors.

Pleasure-motoring and associated sightseeing is the most popular recreational activity. Walking is also popular with between 8% and 10% of visitors likely to take walks of more than 3 kilometres. Angling, caving, canoeing, climbing and hang-gliding are becoming more popular

number of visitors per year to information centres

100 000
50 000

number of day trips per year

1cm width = 1 million

• main tourist centre

The National Park Committee attempts to concentrate activities such as sightseeing and picnicking into a handful of places. These so-called 'honey-pot' locations, such as Malham and Aysgarth, are heavily used by visitors, but help to take pressure off the rest of the park.

8 million people live within 90 minutes travelling time by car from Skipton. The majority of these people live in the nearby West Yorkshire, South Lancashire and Merseyside conurbations.

West Yorkshire

Lancashire, Merseyside, Greater Manchester

Sedbergh · Reeth · Richmond · Hawes · Aysgarth · Buckden · Ingleton · Clapham · Malham · Kettlewell · Settle · Grassington · Bolton Abbey · Skipton

Figure 3.14 Visitor attractions in the Yorkshire Dales national park

Exercise

1 Refer to Figure 3.15 and name the six major land users in national parks.

2 Name the resources that the six major land users require.

3 Read carefully through the land use issues in the Dales national park which are described in Figure 3.16. Then draw a table in your exercise book similar to Table 3.3. Complete your table by putting 'X's where you think that the effects would be harmful. Where the effects are likely to cause little concern put an '0'. The first row in the table has been completed for you. It shows, for example, that farming can harm wildlife, as well as the scenic beauty and man-made features in the landscape. The explanation of this is given in Figure 3.16.

4 Look at the results in your table. Which land uses appear to be a) most harmful, b) least harmful to the national park? How do your results compare with those of others in your class?

Table 3.3   Land use and the Dales' landscape

	Natural beauty				
Land Use	1	2	3	4	5
Farming	X	0	X	X	0
Forestry					
Quarrying					
Recreation					
Military training					
Water supply					

1 = Scenic beauty: valleys, hills, rivers and other natural features.
2 = Landscape character: limestone pavements, scars, dry valleys, caves.
3 = Man-made features: settlements, walls, fields, woodlands.
4 = Wildlife.
5 = Peacefulness.

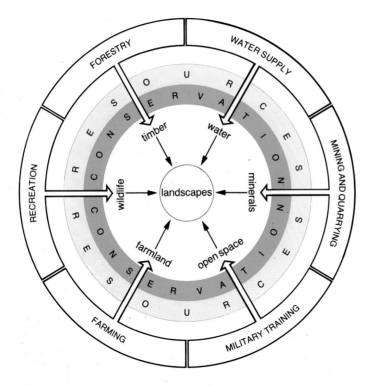

Figure 3.15 National parks: land use, conservation and resources

The issue of quarrying in the Dales

The quarrying of limestone and gritstone occurs on a large scale in the Dales national park. Figure 3.17b shows that quarrying has a massive effect on the landscape, and is impossible to conceal. Moreover, the blasting, crushing, screening, and transport of rock, together with the burning of lime, create noise and dust which extend well beyond the area of the quarry. It may seem strange for the government to create national parks in order to protect their landscapes, only to allow them to be ravaged by quarrying. However, the national parks often contain important mineral resources which are vital to industry and which cannot be obtained elsewhere. In these circumstances, quarrying is permitted because it is in the 'national interest'. In addition, we must not forget that quarrying provides much needed employment for local people in areas where jobs are often difficult to find.

Recreation and leisure

Recreation is largely concentrated in a few centres. No attempt is made to cater for peak demands and provision of car parks, toilets, picnic sites, caravan and camping sites is strictly controlled. Visitors discard litter in the N.P., stray from public footpaths and damage walls. Footpath erosion by pedestrian use is a major problem in the most popular areas eg Malham, Penyghent and Whernside. Surfaced paths have been constructed in several places to limit erosion.

Water supply ■

There are few artificial reservoirs in the park, largely because limestone is permeable. A recent exception was the enlargement of the Grimwith reservoir, with the raising of the dam and the flooding of some farmland. Similar schemes in other parks eg Lake District, have aroused strong opposition in the past.

Forestry

Only 3% of the N.P. is wooded. The natural woodland cover is broadleaf, especially ash and oak. Since 1966, 2500 hectares of commercial conifer forest have been planted and half the area of the park is suitable for afforestation. There have been strong protests against commercial afforestation because:

- conifers change the character of the landscape
- they encroach on open moorland
- they reduce access to the public for recreation
- they dramatically change the habitat for wildlife, reducing the number of species
- on felling, the plantations look unsightly for several years
- much afforestation in the past has been unimaginative, with single conifer species planted in uniform rows

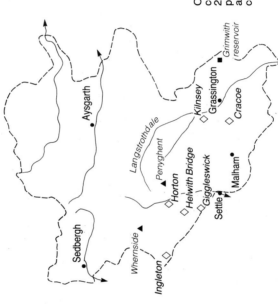

Military Training

Low flying, military aircraft on training exercises within the park are a noisy intrusion.

Farming

Grazing of sheep and cattle dominates farming. Most land is under permanent pasture and rough grazing. Much of the character of the landscape - settlements, fields, walls, barns - has resulted from farming. Issues which arise from farming include:

- there is no control over the design of farm buildings. Often new buildings do not fit in with their surroundings and use modern materials (aluminium, asbestos etc) rather than traditional ones (limestone, gritstone).

- use of chemicals fertilisers to increase the production of hay and silage has destroyed many traditional meadows with their mix of flowering plants. The gradual shift from hay to silage production has also brought about this change.

- artificial drainage of moorland areas, especially on deep peat and bogs, has destroyed some upland habitats for wildlife.

Mineral extraction ◇

Large-scale quarrying of limestone and gritstone is found at 6 sites in the N.P. Quarrying activities destroy the landscape, are noisy, spread dust across the surrounding area and generate heavy lorry traffic. The limestone is chemically pure and is a valuable resource for the steel and chemical industries. However, most limestone is used merely for road fill, which could be extracted from areas outside the N.P. Quarrying is an important source of employment in an area where unemployment is high.

Figure 3.16 Land use issues in the Dales

Figure 3.17a Visitor pressure: Thornton Force, near Ingleton – a popular beauty spot

Figure 3.17b Conflict: limestone quarrying at Cracoe and conservation of the landscapes of the national park

3.17c Modern farm buildings, exempt from planning control, in the Yorkshire Dales national park

Figure 3.17d Visitor pressure: damage to dry stone walls

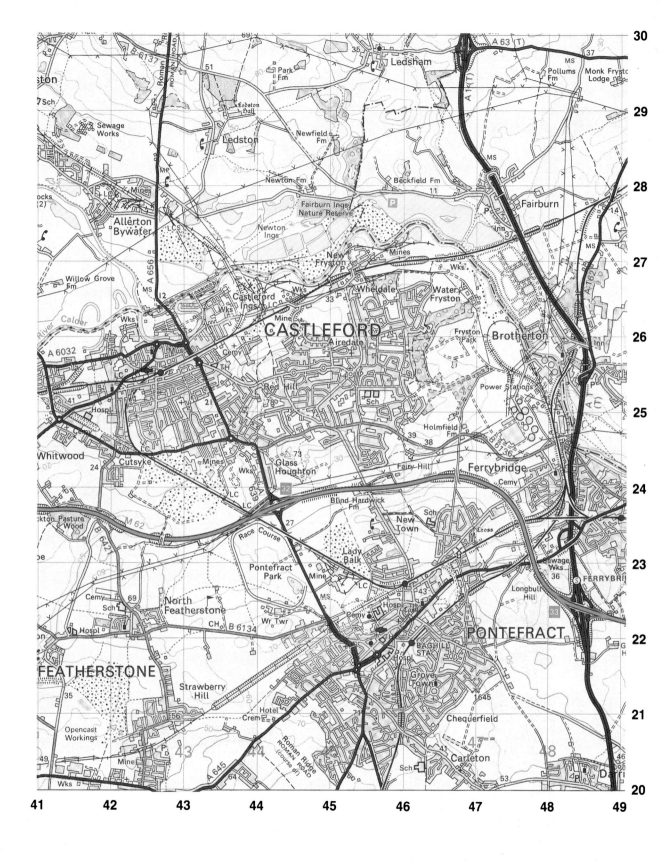

Figure 2.99 The lower Aire Valley, West Yorkshire. Reproduced from the 1986 Ordnance Survey 1:50 000 Landranger map, Crown copyright reserved

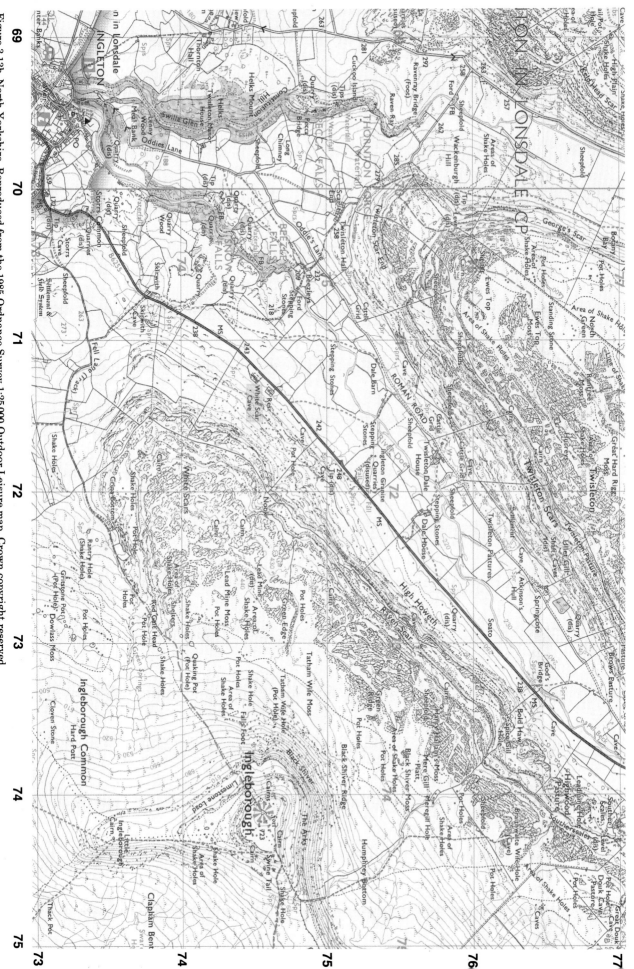

Figure 3.13b North Yorkshire. Reproduced from the 1985 Ordnance Survey 1:25 000 Outdoor Leisure map. Crown copyright reserved

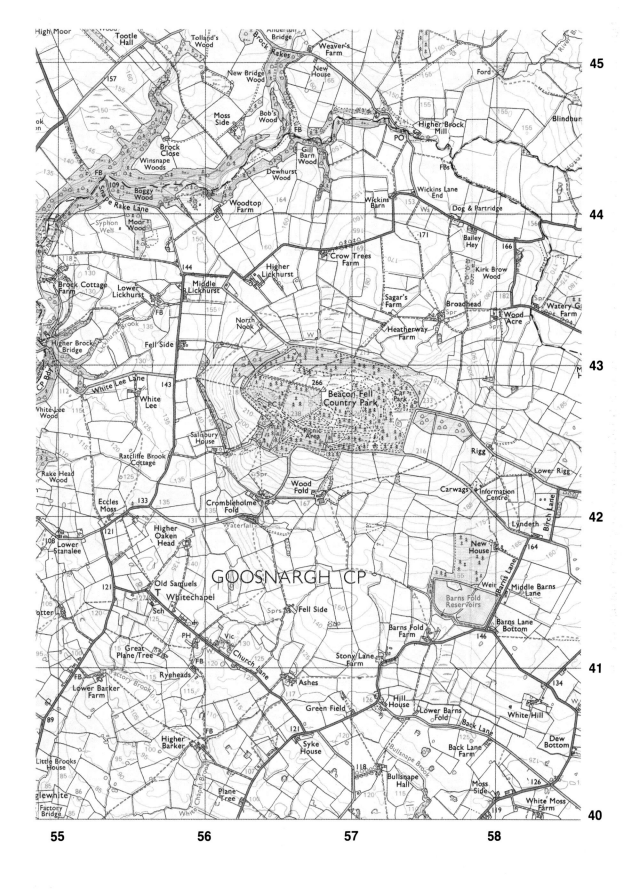

Figure 3.22 Beacon Fell, Lancashire. Reproduced from the 1983 Ordnance Survey 1:25 000 Garstang map, Crown copyright reserved

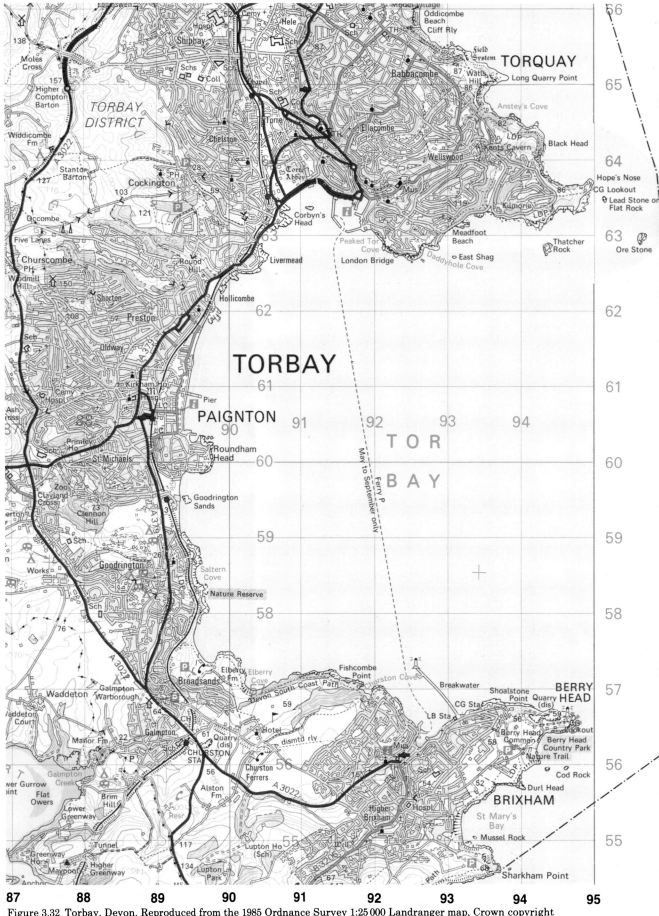

Figure 3.32 Torbay, Devon. Reproduced from the 1985 Ordnance Survey 1:25 000 Landranger map, Crown copyright reserved

Exercise

Read through the newspaper article (Fig. 3.18) from the *Yorkshire Post* which considers the issue of quarrying in the Dales national park, and gives the views of three members of the National Park Committee.

4 Explain in your own words how quarrying in the Dales is linked to the issue of acid rain (look back to page 73 to remind yourself of the details of the acid rain problem).

2 If expansion of quarrying is given the go-ahead, how much extra limestone will be needed from the Dales?

3 What is Councillor Lockyer's attitude towards the expansion of quarrying? Describe the beliefs on which his attitude is based.

4 From the newspaper extract can you suggest a possible reason for the Councillor's view?

5 What is the priority of Councillor Watson on this issue? Describe his attitude and that of Councillor Macare towards any expansion of quarrying.

Acid rain fight needs limestone

Dales quarrying outlook 'horrific'

HORROR was expressed yesterday that 1.6 m tonnes of limestone – required for a trial scheme to remove the cause of acid rain pollution from Britain's power stations – could be quarried in the Yorkshire Dales.

The chairman of the Yorkshire Dales National Park Authority, Coun. John Piper (Upper Dales), told a meeting in Northallerton that the demand for the limestone was an horrific possibility.

But Coun. Keith Lockyer, whose mid-Craven ward includes three major limestone quarries, urged the committee not to be parochial and not to panic about the threat to the landscape.

Every tonne of coal used to fire the Central Electricity Generating Board's power stations contains on average 1.6 per cent sulphur, which is emitted as sulphur dioxide to contribute to acid rain pollution.

By 1997 the CEGB plans to install flue gas desulphurisation at five power stations – including Drax, near Selby; West Burton on the River Trent; and Fiddler's Ferry, near Warrington.

Each of the five would use 320 000 tonnes of high grade limestone – a total of 1.6 m tonnes a year – in a chemical process to extract the sulphur dioxide and leave gypsum as a by-product.

Coun. Lockyer told the committee he had a conscience about sulphur dioxide polluting the atmosphere. He said: "We have a duty as a nation and as a park authority to look at the broader aspects."

"I do feel we can manage our quarries to get this output. We have a duty to achieve a balance. These quarries are a very important part of our Dales economy. Even if it means

using up mineral contents faster, we must go along with it."

Coun. Lockyer claimed a compromise was possible between the demand for limestone and the protection of the Dales landscape. "It is basically a future planning matter," he added.

But Coun. Nigel Watson disagreed. "I am mortified by what Keith Lockyer has had to say", he told the committee. "It is almost as though he was welcoming it into the park."

"We have to put our point forward now. We have to make a pre-emptive strike to make sure everyone knows we are not going to have all this limestone taken out of the Dales Park."

Coun. Watson (Middle Dales) added: "It is arguably one of the ten most beautiful areas of the UK and yet here we are having people say it is all right as long as we take it out by rail."

"Can you imagine the cataclysmic environmental effects it would have on the area? Let's keep things in priority. The harder we press this case and make people sit up and take notice of the potential impact the better."

Coun. Steve Macare (East Central, Harrogate) said there was only one message from the Park authority. "It is one of absolute horror at the possibility of this massive increase in limestone coming from anywhere near this national park."

Members accepted the advice of the National Park officer, Mr. Richard Harvey, to record their concern that any decision on the introduction of anti-pollution measures should not be taken without considering the potential impact of extra quarrying in the Dales.

Figure 3.18 *Yorkshire Post* article on limestone quarrying, 8 May 1987

Figure 3.19 The Lizard: a heritage coast in southern Cornwall. Much of the spectacular coastline of South West England has this protected status

Areas of outstanding natural beauty and heritage coasts

In addition to national parks, there are 36 *areas of outstanding natural beauty* (AONBs) and 38 separate *heritage coasts* (Fig. 3.4) in England and Wales. AONBs are areas of high quality landscape which cover some 10% of the two countries. While the national parks cover areas of rugged upland in the north and west, many AONBs are in the lowlands of southern Britain. The main purpose of AONBs is landscape protection but their growing importance as areas of recreation is now recognised, and today their aims and purposes are very similar to those of national parks.

Stretches of the finest coastline in England and Wales are protected as heritage coasts. This *blue belt* amounts to nearly 1300 kilometres or 29% of the entire coastline of England and Wales (Fig. 3.4). Most heritage coasts coincide with the coastal areas of national parks and AONBs, and extend inland for only a few kilometres.

Exercise

Look closely at Figure 3.4 and complete the following exercise.

1 Find the place where you live on the map and locate the nearest AONB and heritage coast. Visit your local library and try to find out why these areas have been given protected status.

2 Which tourist region has a) the most AONBs, b) the longest heritage coastline, c) the most national parks?

3 Apart from London, which tourist region would you say had a) the best, b) the worst, access to protected landscapes and coasts?

4 Why do you think there are relatively few AONBs in northern England?

5 AONBs are often described as the lowland equivalents of national parks. How many AONBs are largely situated in the lowland tourist regions of the West Midlands, East Midlands, East Anglia, Thames and

Chilterns, South East, and Southern? What
proportion of the total is this? How does
this figure compare to the proportion of
national parks in these lowland regions?

Country parks: 'real countryside on your doorstep'

National parks, AONBs and heritage coasts have been created primarily for
conservation, rather than recreation. Hence they are often found far from the main
centres of population. *Country parks*, on the other hand, are quite different: they
have been designed specifically for recreation, and sited in rural areas *near* large
towns and cities. Here they are conveniently placed for day or half-day trips. Since
1968 more than 150 country parks have been established in England and Wales.
They vary in size from 20 to nearly 2000 hectares. Most of them cover areas of
woodland and grassland, but some have been developed around reservoirs, old
gravel pits, disused railway lines and quarries. Car parks and toilet facilities are
provided, and some have refreshment facilities, picnic sites and information
centres.

Exercise

Figure 3.20 shows the distribution of country
parks in England and Wales. Using this map,
test the idea that country parks cater for the
demand for recreation from people living in
nearby towns and cities. Follow the method
below.

1 Draw circles of 50 kilometre radius, centred
on London, Birmingham, Manchester,
Liverpool, Leeds, Sheffield, Nottingham,
Newcastle-upon-Tyne and Cardiff, and find
the number of country parks within
50 kilometres of these cities.

2 Calculate the percentage of parks within
50 kilometres of these cities, given that in
1987 there were 153 country parks in England
and Wales.

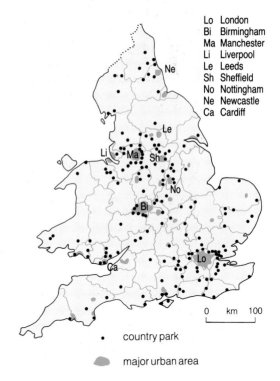

Lo London
Bi Birmingham
Ma Manchester
Li Liverpool
Le Leeds
Sh Sheffield
No Nottingham
Ne Newcastle
Ca Cardiff

0   km   100

• country park

major urban area

Figure 3.20 Country parks in England and Wales

Beacon Fell country park

Beacon Fell country park is a forested hill, covering some 45 hectares in North
Lancashire, on the edge of the Forest of Bowland AONB (Figs 1.5 and 3.21). It was
acquired by Lancashire County Council in 1969 and developed as a country park
for the following reasons.

- It has impressive views over much of the surrounding countryside.
- It is fairly close to the urban centres of Preston, Blackburn and Blackpool.
- It has good transport links with surrounding areas.
- It is a natural gateway to the Forest of Bowland AONB, and by diverting visitors
  from the AONB it would help to reduce visitor pressure and traffic congestion
  there.

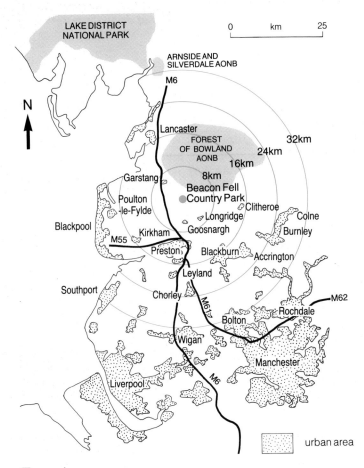

Figure 3.21 Origin of visitors to Beacon Fell country park, Lancashire

Exercise

Look at the 1:25 000 OS extract (Fig. 3.22 in the colour section) which covers Beacon Fell country park.

1 What is the highest point in the park, and what is its grid reference?

2 What type of woodland dominates the park? Name one other type of vegetation which is found in the park.

3 Name *four* facilities in the park which have been provided for visitors.

A number of facilities have been provided at Beacon Fell, including picnic sites, car parks, toilets, waymarked trails and footpaths, and an information centre. The park has proved very popular, especially at weekends and during summer, when up to 800 visitors may be there at any one time. Virtually all visitors travel by car, and two-thirds of them live in the Preston, Blackburn and Blackpool areas (Fig. 3.21). Most trips are half-day outings lasting less than five hours, and on average visitors spend a couple of hours in the park.

Exercise

Figure 3.21 and Table 3.4 provide information on the origin of visitors to Beacon Fell Country Park. Study this information and then attempt the following questions.

1 Why is the proportion of visitors who come from the zone closest to the country park relatively small?

Table 3.4   Distances travelled by visitors to Beacon Fell

distance zone (km)	% visitors
0–8	6.9
9–16	34.9
17–24	39.1
25–32	3.0
over 32	16.1

Figure 3.23 The summit of Beacon Fell, Lancashire

2 Why is the proportion of visitors who travel more than 32 kilometres greater than that from the 25–32 kilometre distance zone?

3 Few people visit Beacon Fell from the Lancaster area. What is the likely explanation for this?

4 There are four factors evident in Figure 3.21 which help to explain the number of visitors to Beacon Fell from places in North West England (some you will have already mentioned in answer to the previous questions). Can you name these factors?

Recreation in the park is dominated by *informal* activities such as exercising dogs, strolling to the summit of the fell, admiring the views, walking along the way-marked trails, picnicking, sunbathing, playing ball games on the grassed areas, and in summer, picking bilberries.

Although Beacon Fell has proved highly popular, it has not been without problems. Vandalism, the dumping of stolen cars, the theft of conifer trees from the plantations, and unauthorised tipping are continual problems. Also the development of informal footpaths by visitors has in places destroyed the vegetation cover, and caused some erosion and gullying.

US national parks

Although national parks are today found throughout the world, they were first established in the USA in the nineteenth century. Yellowstone in Wyoming (Fig. 3.24) was the first in 1872, and was followed by Yosemite and Sequoia in California in 1890. Today there are 39 national parks (as well as numerous national monuments, national recreation areas, and national historic sites) which occupy some 1% of the country's total area. They are managed by the *National Park Service* (NPS), which, apart from employing wardens and rangers, provides visitor facilities such as information centres, camping sites, picnic areas, footpaths and trails.

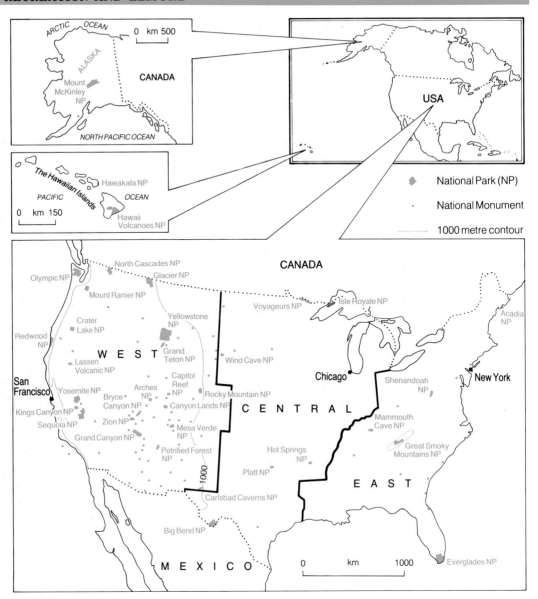

Figure 3.24 National parks and national monuments in the USA

The national parks were created in order to conserve scenery and wildlife, and to make these resources more accessible to the public. All of the parks are areas of outstanding beauty and contain the best examples of America's varied scenery (Fig. 3.25).

In their early days, most parks were remote from the main centres of population and demand in the East. However, with rising standards of living, almost universal car ownership, and more leisure time, some parks have become too popular. Today, one in four Americans visits a national park each year, and the most popular parks face problems of localised overcrowding and damage to landscape and wildlife.

Most parks include large tracts of wilderness. Here the landscape is preserved in its natural condition and there are strict controls over development. The protection of the parks from settlement, farming and industry means that they are used almost exclusively for recreation, especially outdoor activities such as backpacking, climbing, and riding. This has been possible because nearly all national park land is owned by the government. Moreover, as the majority of parks are situated in the West where population densities are low, there is not the same pressure on land from activities such as mining, quarrying, agriculture and water supply as in the UK and western Europe.

Figure 3.25 The Grand Canyon, Arizona: one of the most spectacular national parks in the USA

The Yosemite national park

Yosemite, in California, was one of the first national parks, and is one of the most popular: in 1981 it received $2\frac{1}{2}$ million visitors, a number exceeded only by Great Smoky Mountains, Acadia, Rocky Mountains and Grand Teton national parks (Fig. 3.24). The park covers over 3000 square kilometres, and is nearly twice as large as the Dales national park in the UK. Its principal attraction is the 13-kilometre-long Yosemite Valley (Figs 3.26–3.28) – a glacial trough carved in granite, with sheer rock walls, hanging valleys and waterfalls. Ice age glaciers eroded and over-deepened the Yosemite Valley, leaving smaller tributary, or *hanging valleys*, stranded high above the main valley floor. Today these hanging valleys contain spectacular waterfalls, including Yosemite Falls (739 metres), the highest in North America. Further south at Marisposa Grove, there are stands of giant redwood (sequoia) trees, which are both the largest and oldest living organisms in the world – one is estimated to be nearly 4000 years old. Most of the park is a wilderness area occupying the high country of the Sierra Nevada, which includes several small glaciers around the 3900 metre Mount Lyell.

The main attraction for visitors is the Yosemite Valley, and here a large amount of popular tourist development has been permitted. Accommodation is provided in campsites, inexpensive cabins, and an exclusive hotel complete with tennis courts and heated swimming pool. During the summer, large numbers of visitors place enormous pressure on this area, leading to overcrowding at campsites, traffic congestion, and long queues at cafés, restaurants, gift stores and supermarkets!

The response of the National Park Service has been *de-development*: restrictive measures which limit visitors' freedom, but which help to protect the environment and reduce congestion and pollution. Roads at the eastern end of the Yosemite Valley are restricted to shuttle buses; they follow loop routes (along a one-way traffic system) which take in attractions such as the main waterfalls, hotels, campsites, visitors' centre and trail-heads. In a sense, Yosemite has become a victim of its own popularity, with large numbers of visitors threatening to damage and degrade the environment in the '*honey-pot*' of the Yosemite Valley.

Although the concentration of more than 90% of visitors in the Yosemite Valley creates problems, it relieves pressure on the remaining 99% of the Yosemite national park. The wilderness of the High Sierra attracts few visitors apart from back packers and rock climbers. Even here, access is controlled, and visitors must obtain permits to back-pack and camp overnight in the park. Hunting is banned everywhere.

Figure 3.26 Yosemite Falls, the highest waterfall in North America, and a major attraction for visitors to the Yosemite national park in California

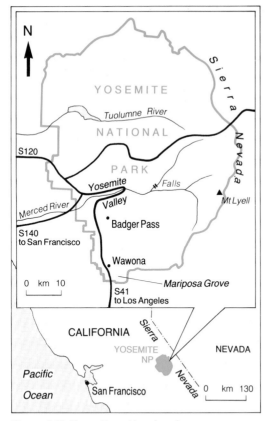

Figure 3.27 Yosemite national park

Exercise

1 Using Figure 3.24, showing the distribution of national parks in the USA, complete Table 3.5.

2 Briefly describe the distribution of national parks in relation to the distribution of population. Would you say that the location of the parks was largely *demand-* or *resource-* oriented?

Table 3.5   Population distribution and national parks in the USA

	population (million)	number of parks
West	41.79	?
Central	67.61	?
East	112.30	?

Figure 3.28 *(right)* The development of the Yosemite Valley

a) Before the ice age

1 Steep-sided V-shaped river valley with narrow floor
2 Winding valley with interlocking spurs

b) During the ice age

1 Glacier-filled valley
2 Valley straightened, deepened and widened
3 Moraine on surface of glacier

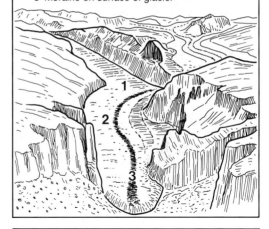

c) After the ice age

1 U-shaped glacial trough
2 Truncated spurs
3 Hanging valley

3 The two most popular parks are the Great Smoky Mountains and Acadia. Try to explain this.

4 Write a paragraph comparing national parks in England and Wales with those in the USA. The following points of comparison could be used: size, purpose, land use, number of visitors, distribution, and land ownership.

5 Explain why the National Park Service (NPS) has, in many respects, an easier task in managing the US national parks, than the National Park Planning Committees in England and Wales.

6 Look at Figure 3.28 showing the modification of the Yosemite Valley by glaciation, and the photograph (Fig. 3.26).
   a Explain briefly how a hanging valley like Yosemite Falls is formed.
   b Suggest how a hanging valley might be useful as a resource other than for recreation and leisure (refer to page 25 if you are unsure.)

Tourism

Tourism in the UK

The main feature of *tourism* is that it involves overnight stays. In order to meet the demand for accommodation, catering, entertainment and travel, a large and expanding *tourist industry* has developed in the UK in recent years. The importance of this industry can be gauged from the following facts.

- Tourism earns the UK more than £7 billion a year.
- 15 million overseas visitors come to the UK each year.
- 4% of all the UK's foreign earnings come from tourism.
- British tourists spend nearly £6 billion a year in the UK.
- The tourist industry provides jobs in hotels, catering, transport, shops and entertainment for some 1.5 million people.
- Tourism is creating new jobs at the rate of 50 000 a year.
- Tourism will continue to grow rapidly in future.

Every region in the UK has its own *tourist board* (Fig. 3.29) to promote its tourist attractions. But, although tourism involves every region, its distribution is uneven. This situation arises because the resources for tourism are much greater in some regions than in others. These resources include natural features, such as climate, coasts, countryside and wildlife; and man-made attractions such as historic buildings, museums, adventure parks and local customs and culture (Fig. 3.30).

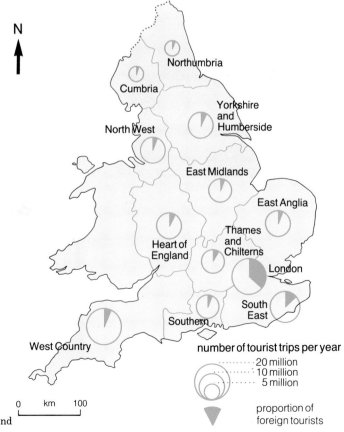

Figure 3.29 Regional tourism in England

Figure 3.30a Tower of London

Figure 3.30b British Museum

Figure 3.30c Stratford-upon-Avon

Figure 3.30d St Paul's Cathedral

Exercise

The regional pattern of tourism in England is shown in Figure 3.29.

1 Which region has: a) the largest total number of tourists, b) the largest number of British tourists, c) the largest number of foreign tourists?

2 For the region which attracted the largest total number of tourists, would you say that the resources for tourism were natural or man-made? How does this compare with the region which attracted the largest number of British tourists? (If you have not visited this region ask those people in your class who have.)

Look carefully at Table 3.6 which lists the most popular tourist attractions in the UK.

3 How many of these tourist attractions are located in London?

Table 3.6 Tourist attractions with over one million visits a year

Museums and art galleries	Historic buildings	Other attractions
British Museum	Westminster Abbey	Blackpool Pleasure Beach
Science Museum	St Paul's Cathedral	Madame Tussaud's
National Gallery	Tower of London	Alton Towers (Staffordshire)
Natural History Museum	Canterbury Cathedral	Bradgate Park (Leicestershire)
Jewel House	York Minster	Wickstead Park (Northamptonshire)
Victoria & Albert Museum		Thorpe Park (Surrey)
Tate Gallery	**Gardens**	Box Hill Country Park (Surrey)
Royal Academy of Arts	Kew	
Wildlife attractions		
London Zoo		

4 Describe how your answer to **3** helps explain the importance of London as a tourist centre, as shown in Figure 3.29?

5 Make a list of the attractions you have visited and add a note to show whether you visited them as a day-tripper or as a tourist.

6 If you were allowed to visit one of these attractions on a school trip, which one would you choose? Write a paragraph explaining in some detail your choice, and compare it with those of other members of your class. (Incidentally, the single most popular attraction is Blackpool Pleasure Beach which has over 6 million visitors a year!)

7 All of the attractions listed in Table 3.6, except one, are man-made features. Can you find the exception? (If you are not sure, look back to page 147.)

With rising living standards, cheap air travel and more leisure time, tourism has grown into an *international* industry. In 1985 more than 15 million foreign tourists visited the UK, which is most popular with tourists from the USA, France and West Germany. They spent a total of £5.5 billion and two-thirds of them stayed in London. Meanwhile, one in three British tourists now take a holiday abroad every year. As the popularity of foreign holidays increases (Fig. 3.31), traditional British seaside resorts like Blackpool, Bournemouth and Torbay, are finding it increasingly difficult to attract British holiday-makers. Spain is easily the most popular destination among Britons taking holidays abroad (Fig. 3.42); indeed three out of every five foreign holidays spent by British tourists are in the Mediterranean Basin.

Exercise

Tourists choose a holiday location for many reasons. Some are listed below:

natural scenery	easy to get to
beaches	peace and quiet
places of interest	evening entertainment
cost	good accommodation
uncrowded	cleanliness
sun	friendly local people

1 Using your own values, rank the attractions given above from 1 (most important) to 12 (least important).

2 Taking account of your ranking in **1**, in which of the following countries would you most like to spend a holiday: France, Italy, Norway, Spain, Switzerland, West Germany? Explain your choice, and describe the kind of holiday you would spend there.

3 In 1985, the percentage of Britons holidaying abroad who stayed in these six countries were: France (10%), Italy (6%), Norway (1%), Spain (36%), Switzerland (2%) and West Germany (5%). Calculate similar percentages using the first choice of everyone in your class, and compare them with the actual figures. Are they similar? If so, find out what makes some countries more popular than others?

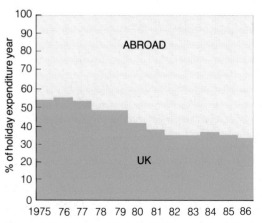

Figure 3.31 % expenditure by UK tourists in UK and abroad 1975–86 (for holidays lasting four days or more)

Torbay: the English Riviera

Torbay, on the coast of South Devon (Fig. 3.33), is a typical British holiday resort. It consists of three separate centres – Torquay (the largest), Paignton and Brixham – and is situated within the West Country, which is the UK's leading tourist region (Fig. 3.29). On average one in four Britons who take a holiday in the UK choose the West Country, though it is far less popular with foreign tourists.

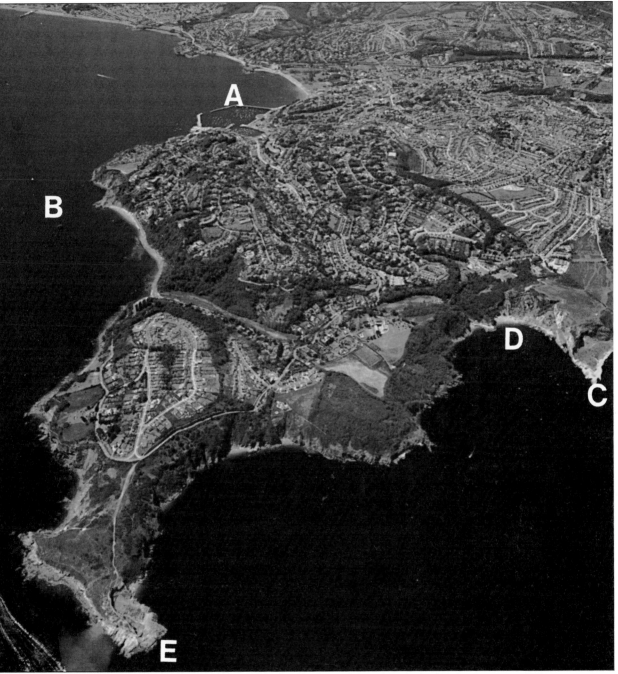

Figure 3.33 Torquay

Exercise

Study the OS map (Fig. 3.32) and the air photograph (Fig. 3.33) of Torquay and complete the exercises below.

1 In which direction was the camera pointing when the photograph was taken?

2 Give the 4-figure grid reference of the harbour at A, and the six-figure grid reference of the island at B.

3 Name the headland at C, and the bay at D.

4 Suggest three reasons why the coast between D and E is largely unattractive to tourists.

5 Why is the path which leads to the headland at E an important tourist attraction?

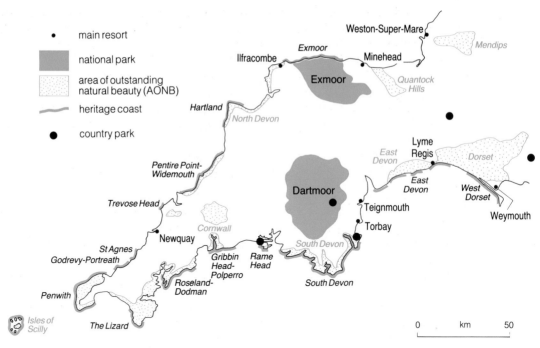

Figure 3.34 Resources for tourism in the West Country

Torbay is the largest tourist centre in the West Country. Well over a million tourists stay there each year; among British seaside resorts, only Blackpool and Brighton are more popular. The attractions of Torbay are both natural and man-made. There are 40 kilometres of coastline, with 18 bathing beaches, sandy bays, and rugged cliffs. Compared with other British resorts, the summer months are warm and sunny, and the mild winter allows exotic palm trees to grow outdoors – this is why Torbay is advertised as 'The English Riviera'. Figure 3.34 shows that Torbay also has beautiful countryside close at hand, most notably the Dartmoor national park, the South Devon AONB, and the South Devon heritage coast.

There is no shortage of man-made tourist attractions. As in other large resorts, there are theatres, cinemas, discos, leisure centres, a zoo, a steam railway, aquaria and a range of sporting facilities from sea angling to golf. Torbay tries to appeal to a wide cross-section of holiday-makers, and provide entertainment in the evenings and when it rains.

Exercise

Study the 1:50 000 OS map extract of Torbay (Fig. 3.32 in the colour section).

Make a list of two natural and man-made tourist attractions that you can find on the map. Give the six figure grid reference of each attraction.

Problems facing tourism in Torbay

Two major problems face traditional seaside resorts: the decline in their popularity with British holiday-makers; and seasonal unemployment.

The popularity of British seaside resorts (Fig. 3.35) with British holiday-makers, has been declining for many years. Traditionally, resorts like Torbay have catered for long holidays, lasting a week or more. However, countries such as Spain, Italy,

Greece and Jugoslavia are able to offer similar holidays at competitive prices *and* guarantee sunshine. Furthermore, the provision of new tourist accommodation and entertainment facilities in these countries has kept pace with the demand in a way that few British seaside resorts have been able to match. Today, Britons take 15 million holidays abroad, and this trend is set to continue.

Seasonal unemployment has always been a problem in Torbay, with most visitors concentrated in the height of the season between June and September (Fig. 3.36). Of the 17 000 people employed directly by tourism, only 6500 have permanent, all-year-round jobs.

With the livelihoods of so many people at stake, it is essential that Torbay responds to these problems. Some of the solutions are listed below.

- Depend less on long holidays, and encourage shorter holidays of two or three days. More and more people are taking short holidays in addition to their main holiday, and these holidays are usually spent in the UK.
- Encourage more foreign tourists to visit Torbay (Torbay already has several foreign language schools).
- Expand the role of Torbay as a conference centre: conferences provide valuable trade in the off-peak period.
- Invest more in both existing and new holiday accommodation (eg hotels, apartments, guest houses), and in new attractions such as leisure centres, marinas, swimming pools and sports halls.
- Offer more special-interest holidays, based on people's hobbies, interests and sport (eg rambling, painting, golf). This type of holiday has shown rapid growth in recent years.

Exercise

1 What is the main disadvantage of Torbay as a conference centre and as a place for short holidays, compared with Blackpool and Brighton? To help you answer, make a list of the major urban centres from Figure 3.35 which are situated within 200 kilometres of Torquay, Blackpool and Brighton.

2 If *you* were given the task of attracting more young tourists to Torbay, what kind of facilities would you provide? If these facilities were provided, and the cost were the same, would you be persuaded to spend a week's holiday in Torbay rather than in Spain or Italy? Explain your answer.

Figure 3.35 Most popular seaside resorts and major urban centres in the UK

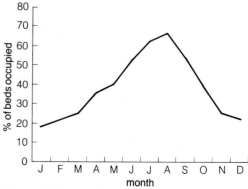

Figure 3.36 Seasonality of tourism in the West Country

3 Study the 1:50 000 OS extract of Torbay and the resources available for recreation. Name the resources and suggest possible special-interest holidays that could make use of them.

Beach pollution at UK resorts: a national scandal?

The UK's beaches are amongst the most polluted in Europe. They are fouled by litter, oil, industrial waste, and even radioactive substances. However, the biggest single cause of pollution is untreated sewage. Although it is usual for raw sewage to be discharged directly into the sea, there is little chance of the sewage fouling beaches as long as the outfalls extend well beyond the low-water mark. Once in the sea, sewage is quickly diluted and made harmless by the action of sunlight, oxygen, salt and bacteria.

Problems arise when untreated sewage is discharged either *on* or *near* the shore. There are more than 80 popular bathing beaches in England and Wales where this occurs (Fig. 3.37). The result is sewage solids washed up on beaches and high levels of bacteria in the water. Sewage is not merely unpleasant, it is also a health risk, particularly to children. Admittedly the danger of catching a serious illness such as polio or typhoid is extremely small, but swimming in polluted water often causes stomach upsets, and bacteria in raw sewage can infect cuts and cause eye inflammation. In any event, polluted beaches are bad news for the tourist industry.

The issue of polluted beaches led to a European Community (EC) ruling in 1976 that each member state had to name the beaches where bathing was popular, and these beaches had to meet EC standards by 1985. However, the UK government named only 27 out of its 600 beaches where bathing takes place regularly. Among the notable omissions were Blackpool, Brighton, Eastbourne, Great Yarmouth and Morecambe! Even with only 27 beaches to bring up to standard, six failed the EC hygiene tests in 1986. Indeed, in 1986 the government monitored pollution levels on 369 of Britain's most popular beaches and found that half failed to reach the required standard.

beaches failing to meet EC hygiene standards (ie high levels of bacteria from sewage)

untreated sewage is discharged at or above the low-water mark

Figure 3.37 Beach pollution in England and Wales

Most people would agree that the present state of the UK's beaches is unacceptable, and that governments in the past have tried to get round EC rules. The reason why pollution has continued is simply one of money. It is expensive to give sewage even basic treatment or to build long outfalls well beyond the low-water mark. Even so, in 1984 the Royal Commission on Environmental Pollution said that this was precisely what should be done. Now the government has announced plans to spend £300 million over the next three years to tackle the problem. However, most experts believe that it will need at least three times this amount to keep all sewage away from the beaches.

A POLICY FOR SEWAGE

Several generations have been reared on the assumption that the beaches of Britain were cold — but clean and good for you, like freezing showers and cabbage. As the summer sun beats down from the pierhead however, the reverse is now beginning to look true.

Like many of the other assumptions which once underpinned our national sense of confidence, the purity of our coasts and coastal waters owed much to the energy and diligence of Victorian engineers. We travelled on their railways, sent prisoners to their jails, recovered in their hospitals and danced over the pebbles of Brighton beach to bathe in unadulterated brine — a tribute to their science of sewage disposal.

Or so we thought. In fact, even in their day, Victorian schemes for disposing of sewage at sea were primitive. Now too many of them have been overtaken by a combination of old age and increased populations. In many cases, raw sewage is said to have been pumped into rivers, by-passing treatment plants which cannot cope. In others, the outfall pipes which carry effluent from coastal towns into the sea, are too short to do the job effectively. The tides on which the Victorians depended to disperse and dispose of the waste in the waters around Britain's coasts can no longer be relied upon to do so. They dump it on the beaches or let it stagnate offshore — giving rise

to experiences like that of the lady, quoted in the Commons the other day, who found herself swimming through untreated sewage at Seaford.

Greenpeace whose research vessel, the *Beluga*, completes a two-month survey of the country's coasts and estuaries today, complains also of industrial pollution caused by firms which discharge metals into the waters of local authorities — whose sewage farms are too limited to deal with them. As industrial rivers pour into the North and Irish Seas, these add to the accumulation of local waste, endangering marine life and, for all we know, ourselves.

From regarding Britain as one of the most hygiene-minded nations in Europe, we must face up to the uncomfortable fact that this is no longer necessarily so. A £30m scheme has been launched to correct the situation at Blackpool, that most English of English resorts. Now Mr William Waldegrave, the Minister for the Environment, has announced that 80 schemes are in the pipeline. These are likely to cost a total of £300m during the next five years as water authorities try to grapple with the problem. But the Coastal Anti-Pollution League says that this represents only half the investment needed to clean up the country's beaches.

Britain compares badly with countries like France and Italy when it officially releases details of conditions at only 27

beaches. France monitors 1,498 coastal resorts and 1,366 inland towns, while Italy 3,308 on the coast and 57 inland. The reason for this is that Whitehall concerns itself only with beaches on which as many as 500 might be in the water at any one time — and it is undeniably true that unlike the Mediterranean powers, this is hardly a country to attract the international set to its coasts. But the disparity is so great that it suggests either complacency or disingenuousness on the part of successive governments here.

The present Government is trying to correct this, and the result of a survey of 350 beaches should be released next Spring at the end of a two-year operation. Preliminary results suggest, according to Mr Waldegrave, that up to half of them will be found to come up to European Community standards. But this hardly merits his comment of "quite encouraging".

Better understanding of the chemistry involved and the availability of new technology now enable authorities to introduce far more effective means of disposing of sewage in deep water. Water authorities may shrink from the prospect of heavy capital outlays, especially if privatization lies ahead. But concern is rising to the extent that the state of our coastline could swiftly come to be regarded as a national scandal unless they act soon, effectively and with Government backing.

Figure 3.38 Extract from *The Times*, 25 July 1986

Figure 3.39 Raw sewage discharged onto the beach at Ladye Bay, near Clevedon, Avon

Exercise

Read through the newspaper extract which appeared in *The Times* in July 1986 (Fig. 3.38).

1 Why are the Victorian sewage systems found in Britain's resorts no longer adequate?

2 Apart from pollution from sewage, what other source of pollution is mentioned in the article?

3 How do Britain's beaches compare with those in France and Italy?

4 What did the Minister for the Environment say about a recent survey which indicated that half of Britain's beaches met EC standards? What is the attitude of the article towards the Minister's comment?

5 State your views on the issue of beach pollution. Would you be prepared to pay higher taxes in order to clean up the beaches?

Tourism in Spain: 'everything under the sun'

If you have ever spent a holiday abroad, it is very likely that you will have visited Spain: Spain attracts one in every three Britons who take a foreign holiday. These people are part of the 43 million foreign tourists who visit Spain (and the Balearic and Canary Islands, both of which belong to Spain) every year.

The attraction of Spain to tourists from northern Europe is summed up in the Spanish National Tourist Office's slogan 'everything under the sun'. Millions head south on 'package holidays' which provide low-cost air travel and accommodation. For one or two weeks they exchange the cool, damp, cloudy weather that we call summer, for the certainty of blue skies, high temperatures, and, of course, a sun tan! (Fig. 3.40). Majorca and the Mediterranean coast are the most popular locations (Fig. 3.41); Majorca alone accounting for a third of all holidays taken by foreign visitors. On arrival at the airport these 'parachute tourists' are taken by bus to nearby resorts, where most spend the entire holiday. The main attraction by day is sunbathing on the beach, while in the evenings entertainment is provided by the many restaurants, pubs, discos and night clubs.

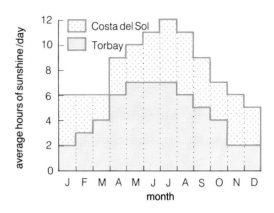

Figure 3.40 Sunshine on the Costa del Sol (Spain) and Torbay (UK)

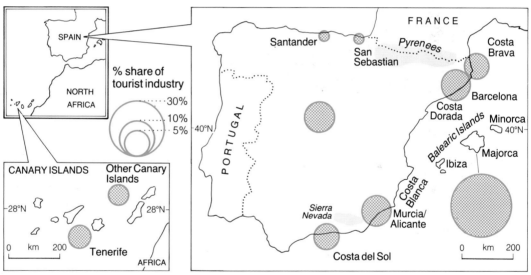

Figure 3.41 Major tourist centres in Spain

Spain's mass tourist industry really started in the 1950s and 1960s with the introduction of cheap air travel and longer holidays for workers. During this period the Spanish government encouraged the rapid growth of the industry, with minimal planning controls. The speed of development and its haphazard nature led to a number of problems:

- *Strip development* in the most popular areas, with hotels and apartments forming a continuous built-up zone along miles of coastline.
- Multi-storey buildings along sea-fronts, which block the light and sea views from buildings further inland.
- Low density villa development sprawling across hillsides facing the sea.
- Lack of essential services such as water supply and sewage treatment, and inadequate roads.

Now the boom years of tourism are over, and any future growth is likely to be much slower (Fig. 3.43). The government is at last turning its attention to more *thoughtful* tourism which will protect the environment, provide adequate services,

Figure 3.42 Torremolinas on the Costa del Sol is one of Spain's most popular resorts. Note the strip development of multi-storey apartments and hotels only a few metres away from the beach

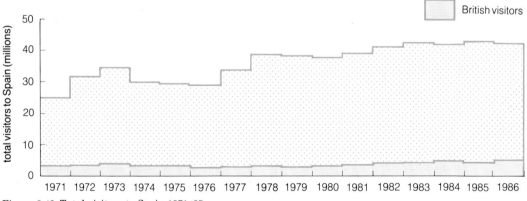

Figure 3.43 Total visitors to Spain 1971–85

and spread the industry to regions outside Mediterranean Spain, as well as more evenly throughout the year. Already stricter building regulations have been adopted, and minimum standards for the provision of essential services such as water supply, sewage treatment and transport have been laid down. The government is also providing money for winter sports complexes in the Pyrenees and Sierra Nevada and wants to break the monopoly of sun/beach tourism by encouraging special-interest holidays based on activities such as golf, water sports and even hunting. Finally, the problem of unemployment in tourism during the off-peak season is being tackled by offering cheap winter holidays to pensioners to take advantage of the mild climate at that time of year.

Exercise

1 Use an atlas and Figure 3.41 to match the following resorts with the major Spanish tourist regions listed below: Alicante, Benidorm, Lloret del Mar, Malaga, Marbella, Tarragona, Torremolinas.
    Costa del Sol
    Costa Brava
    Costa Dorado
    Costa Blanca

2 Visit your local travel agent and try to obtain a copy of a holiday brochure of a large tour operator, such as Thomson or Clarkson, which sells holidays in Spain. You will find a large number of holidays advertised for Mediterranean Spain, the Balearics and the Canary Islands, with information on prices, accommodation, air travel, tourist attractions, climate and so on. Imagine that you have £300 to spend on a holiday in Spain. Using the information in the brochure:
a Choose a holiday region and a resort.
b Decide when you would take the holiday (prices vary at different times of the year) and the type of accommodation you would choose (self-catering, half- or full-board).
c Find the nearest airport in the UK where you could fly from. How long would the flight take? Name the airport where you would land in Spain.
d Describe what the resort has to offer which appeals to you, including the climate. (You might like to include some photographs from the brochure.)
e Describe any tourist attractions in the surrounding area that could be visited.
f Would you prefer to spend your £300 on a holiday in Torbay (see previous section) instead of Spain? Explain your choice in a paragraph.

Tourism in Switzerland: the heart of Europe

Tourism is a leading Swiss industry, employing 260 000 people in the peak holiday season. The main attraction is the magnificent scenery of the Alps. Every year over 7 million foreign tourists visit Switzerland, and contribute over 10% of the country's total income.

Switzerland is centrally situated between northern and southern Europe, and for centuries the only direct route to the Mediterranean lay across its high Alpine passes. In the nineteenth century it was mainly the British who discovered Switzerland as a holiday playground, and were the first to scale many of the Alpine peaks.

Although Switzerland is a small country, barely half the size of Scotland, there is great variety in its scenery. There are three main regions: the Jura, the Central Plateau and the Alps (Fis 3.44–3.45). In the north the Jura mountains cover 10% of the country. Compared to the Alps they are modest in height, but the forest-covered limestone ridges, cut through in places by spectacular gorges, make this a very attractive area. The Central Plateau, stretching from Lake Geneva to Lake Constance, is covered by great thicknesses of glacial deposits, and with an average height of only 580 metres, has a relatively mild climate. It contains two-thirds of Switzerland's population, most of its large towns and industry, and best farmland. Old cities like Geneva, Zurich and Bern are popular tourist centres in their own right. However, it is the third region – the Alps – for which Switzerland is most famous. They cover 60% of the country and average 1700 metres in height. Over a hundred summits, including the Matterhorn and Jungfrau, rise to around 4000 metres. The Alps are *young fold mountains* which are still rising at the present day; and everywhere, the Alpine landscape bears the clear imprint of recent glaciation. Indeed in many places glaciers are still active today.

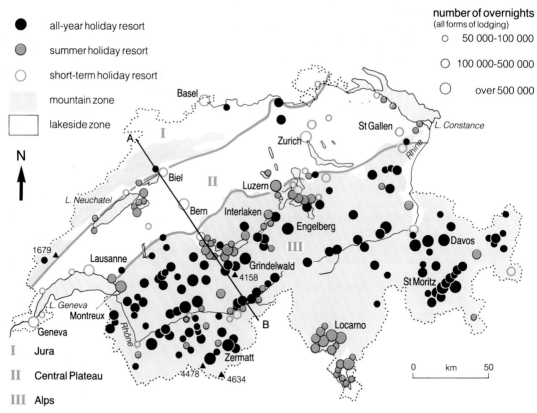

Figure 3.44a Distribution of tourism in Switzerland

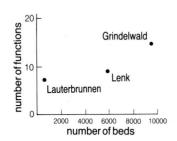

Figure 3.44b Size of Swiss resorts and range of functions

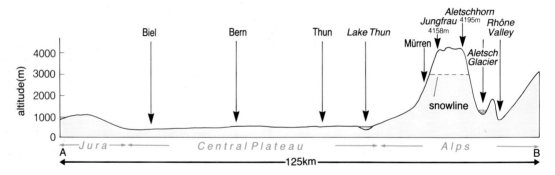

Figure 3.45 North-south relief section across Switzerland

Tourism in the Bernese Oberland

Swiss tourism is an all-year-round industry. About one-third of all foreign tourists visit the country in the winter months (Fig. 3.46) principally on skiing holidays. Most ski resorts are small centres situated in mountainous areas like the Bernese Oberland. Accommodation is mainly in chalets and in holiday apartments for between 500 and 1000 visitors. Some, such as Mürren (Fig. 3.47) are only accessible by cable car. Chair lifts and cable cars transport the skiers to the ski slopes.

The boom in skiing in Switzerland in the 1960s and 1970s led to the development of many new lifts and slopes. Although this provided employment and prosperity in the ski resorts, the environment suffered: soils were badly eroded, alpine plants destroyed, wildlife disrupted, and roads became congested with cars. Today the Swiss authorities are trying to limit any further expansion in order to protect the environment. But in the Alpine region, where tourism either directly or indirectly employs over half the population there is anger and concern that such restrictions will not only create unemployment, but threaten the survival of villages which depend wholly on tourism.

Tourism remains important in these resorts during the summer months when sightseeing and hiking take over as the main activities. Some of the larger mountain resorts like Grindelwald and Wengen (Fig. 3.47) have facilities for all-year-round tourism including tennis courts, cinemas, swimming pools and even golf courses. Tourist centres in the valleys, such as Interlaken and Thun, which lack the altitude and slopes necessary for skiing, are mainly summer resorts. In the Bernese Oberland these resorts are clustered around the shores of Lakes Thun and Brienz. Several are small, historic towns, with old churches, castles and museums. Access to the lakes gives tourists a wide choice of activities, including steamer trips, sailing, wind-surfing and water-skiing.

Figure 3.46 *(right)* Foreign tourists in Switzerland

Figure 3.47 *(below)* Tourist resorts in the Bernese Oberland

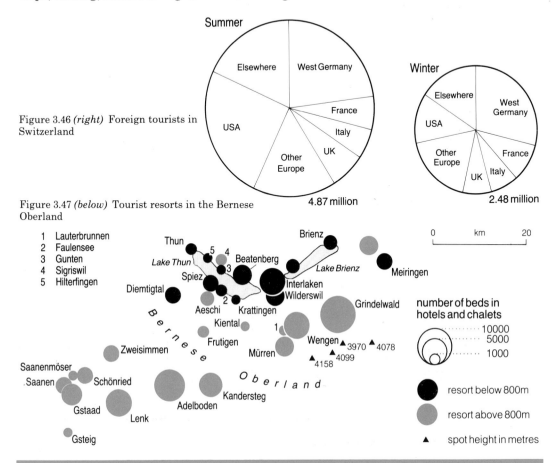

Table 3.7   Size of resort and range of tourist functions

Mountain resorts	No. of beds	Functions	Valley resorts	No. of beds	Functions
Adelboden	7700	14	Brienz	1400	10
Aeschi	1000	3	Diemtigtal	1640	6
Beatenberg	2800	6	Faulensee	530	6
Grindelwald	9450	15	Frutigen	1000	11
Gstaad	3000	16	Gunten	450	8
Hasliberg	2100	4	Hilterfingen	410	7
Kandersteg	3500	14	Interlaken	4950	20
Kiental	440	2	Krattingen	290	5
Lenk	5990	9	Lauterbrunnen	700	8
Mürren	1900	8	Meiringen	1840	14
Saanen	1500	9	Ringenberg	1040	4
Saanenmöser	370	4	Spiez	810	14
Schönried	1780	6	Thun	870	20
Sigriswil	495	6	Wilderswil	1600	5
Wengen	4700	9			
Zweisimmen	1880	7			

Exercise

1 Using the information in Table 3.7 calculate the average number of beds and different tourist functions for a) mountain resorts, b) valley resorts.

2 For the two types of resort, divide the average number of beds by the average number of different functions. In relation to size, which type of resort has the greater range of functions?

3 Plot the information for mountain resorts as a scattergraph (like Fig. 3.44b) with size of resort (ie number of beds) on the horizontal axis, and number of different tourist functions on the vertical axis. What happens to the number of functions as size increases? Try to explain this.

4 Copy the paragraph below, inserting the missing words:
Most mountain resorts, considering their size, have a _____ range of tourist functions. Although these resorts are usually involved in tourism throughout the year, many smaller ones are geared towards skiing in _____ . The nature of skiing means that there is limited demand for other recreational activities, particularly during the _____ . Furthermore, the relative _____ of many mountain resorts means that: a) they attract few _____ who might boost the range of tourist activities, b) they must provide accommodation for visitors which tends to overstate their size.
day-trippers, narrow, day, isolation, winter

5 Write a similar paragraph in your exercise book to explain the main features of tourist centres at lower altitude, in the valleys.

Transport and communications in Switzerland

The Swiss government recognises the importance of a modern transport network to the tourist industry. Since 1960 work has been progressing on a national highway system which includes 1500 kilometres of motorway. In the Alps, the opening of the St Gotthard road tunnel in 1980 (Fig. 3.48a) gave Switzerland a third, year-round road link with Italy.

Swiss railways are modern and fully electrified. There are three north–south rail tunnels through the Alps. They are followed by spectacular routes which are tourist attractions in their own right. In 1982 the Furka rail tunnel was completed after 10 years' work, and has greatly improved east–west communications across the Alps. In the tourist areas, cog-and-rack railways, cable railways and hundreds of aerial cableways carry visitors into the mountains. Recently several of these areas have been connected directly by rail services to Zurich international airport.

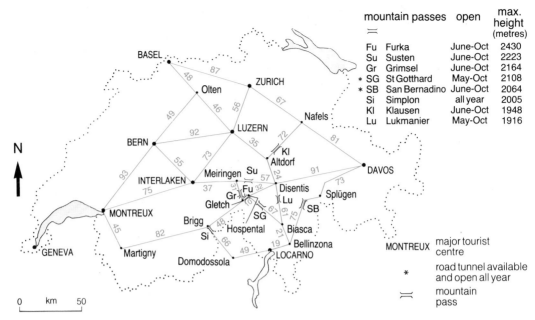

mountain passes		open	max. height (metres)
Fu	Furka	June–Oct	2430
Su	Susten	June–Oct	2223
Gr	Grimsel	June–Oct	2164
* SG	St Gotthard	May–Oct	2108
* SB	San Bernadino	June–Oct	2064
Si	Simplon	all year	2005
Kl	Klausen	June–Oct	1948
Lu	Lukmanier	May–Oct	1916

MONTREUX major tourist centre

* road tunnel available and open all year

mountain pass

Figure 3.48a Transport and tourism in Switzerland

Figure 3.48b Ferpecle glacier in the Valais

In addition to Zurich, there are international airports at Geneva and Basel. Together these airports handle 15 million passengers a year and provide direct flights to all major European cities.

Figure 3.48c Skiing in the Prattigau Valley, the Grisons

Figure 3.48d Bern, historic town and the Swiss capital

Exercise

Figure 3.48a is a simplified road map of Switzerland, which shows distance in kilometres between key places and the main Alpine passes. Imagine that you are planning to spend a fortnight in July touring Switzerland by car. You want to start and finish your tour in Basel, and visit the seven other major tourist centres on the map (Bern, Davos, Interlaken, Locarno, Luzern, Montreux and Zurich).

1 Plan the shortest route between these places and make a note of it in your exercise book.

2 Calculate the total distance of your route and make a note of the Alpine passes that you crossed.

3 Compare the distance of your route with those of others in your class.

4 Suppose that you were to make the same trip in April. How would your route differ and how long would it be? (Clue: look at the dates that the Alpine passes are open and the location of the two road tunnels in Fig. 3.48a.)

5 In 1987 a new motorway link between Zurich and the ski resorts around Davos (Fig. 3.48a) was completed. Tourist numbers are expected to increase by 10% as a consequence. What do you think is the likely attitude towards this development by a) the tourist board in the Davos region, b) environmentalists. If you are unsure, re-read the section on skiing in Switzerland.

Barbados: tourism and development

Barbados is the most easterly of the Caribbean islands (Fig. 3.49) and is similar in size to the Isle of Man. It is situated just 13 degrees north of the equator and has a warm climate throughout the year (Table 3.8). The tropical climate, long coastline,

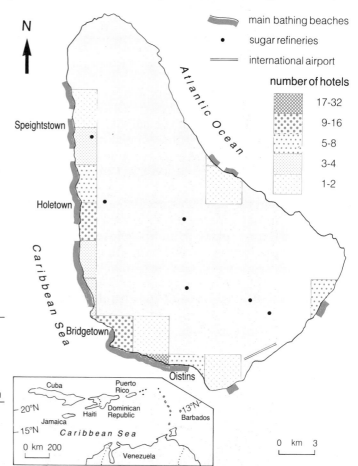

Table 3.8   Barbados: climate

Warmest month: July 27.2°C
Coldest month: January 25.0°C

Wettest month: October 190.8 mm
Driest month: March 37.1 mm

Mean annual precipitation: 1296 mm

Figure 3.49 Barbados: pattern of tourism

Figure 3.50a Fishing boats on the rugged windward (eastern) coast of Barbados

and beautiful scenery are the basis for the island's tourist industry (Fig. 3.50). The coastline is one of great contrasts. The northern and eastern coasts are on the windward side of the island. Here, the prevailing north east trade winds generate powerful Atlantic breakers, which have carved out rugged cliffs, with caves, arches and stacks. The western and southern coasts occupy the sheltered leeward side of the island, where there are extensive beaches, and calm warm waters, ideal for bathing.

In the last 20 years the development of tourism has been carefully planned around a number of tourist zones. The west coast has been zoned for higher-priced luxury hotels, while the south and south east coasts for medium to low-priced apartments. Meanwhile, the rugged Atlantic coast is to be preserved for its scenic qualities, and may be designated as a national park.

Tourism is now the island's leading economic activity. In 1955 there were only 15 000 visitors to the island; in 1986 there were 370 000 long-stay visitors, and 147 000 short-stay visitors (mainly from cruise-liners). There are over 150 hotels, guesthouses and apartments, providing 14 000 beds. Overall tourism directly employs around 16% of the workforce, and it contributes more to the island's economy than both manufacturing and the sugar industry together.

Tourism has also benefited the island's communications. For instance in 1961 the deep water harbour at Bridgetown was opened, allowing large Caribbean cruise-liners to include a stop at Barbados in their schedules. The international airport was up-graded in 1980, and there are now direct flights from several major cities, including London, New York, Toronto, Frankfurt, Brussels and Rio de Janeiro. (See Fig. 3.51.)

Figure 3.50b The sheltered leeward (west) coast of Barbados. White coral beaches and palm trees are a typical scene in western parts of the island

Tourist development has, however, brought with it a number of problems, which are outlined below. Most of them stem from the island's smallness and relative isolation.

- There are only a limited number of suitable sites for tourist development which are mainly concentrated along the south and west coasts. In some places, the high density of hotel building along the coast has effectively screened-off inland areas from the sea.
- Barbados has only limited resources of its own, and must therefore rely heavily on imported food for tourists, and foreign investment in hotels, apartments and other tourist facilities. As a result much of the profit from tourism 'leaks' overseas.
- Tourism caters almost exclusively for international tourists. Unlike tourism in larger countries, there is little domestic tourism on Barbados. The island is so small that local people can easily visit tourist spots from home, without over-night stays. The absence of domestic tourists, and the reliance on foreign tourists means that a) the scale of the tourist industry remains fairly small, and b) the success of tourism depends on economic conditions in developed countries, especially in the USA, Canada and the UK, over which Barbados has no control.

- Like other small tropical and sub-tropical islands, the Barbados tourist industry depends heavily on the three S's – sand, sun and sea. Although there are local folk festivals, craft and duty-free shops, many sporting activities and sightseeing, the range of tourist attractions on the island is small compared to other major tourist regions.
- Being isolated, holidays are formally organised by foreign tour operators, mainly as packages. Tourists arrive by air, and are content to remain at their hotel and beach. There is not much scope for informal tourist development (eg caravan sites, camping, small guesthouses, cafés, pubs, small restaurants) which tends to benefit local people more.

Exercise

1 Tourism, based on the three S's, is an all-year-round activity in Barbados. What is the main reason for this?

2 With reference to Figure 3.49, find out how far it is between the most northerly and southerly points on Barbados.

3 The supply of land for tourist development along the coast is limited by two factors. One is the small size of the island. What is the other?

4 Look at Figure 3.49, and using *only* the information it provides, explain the distribution of tourism in Barbados.

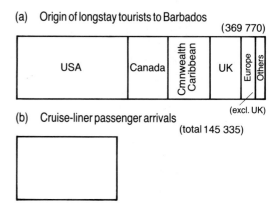

(a) Origin of longstay tourists to Barbados (369 770)

USA | Canada | Cmnwealth Caribbean | UK | Europe | Others

(excl. UK)

(b) Cruise-liner passenger arrivals (total 145 335)

Figure 3.51 Origin of tourists, and cruise-liner arrivals in Barbados

Kenya: an image of Africa

Tourism is Kenya's fastest growing industry, attracting 450 000 visitors in 1986. It is worth nearly £200 million a year, and after coffee, it is Kenya's main source of foreign currency. Around 11 000 people find work in accommodation and catering for tourists. With Kenyan incomes barely averaging £200 a year, and a population growth rate which is the highest in the world, the Kenyan government has been keen to develop the country's tourist resources.

Planning for tourism started in the 1960s with the establishment of a Ministry of Tourism. Hotels, game lodges, and tourist roads have been built, and today there are 15 000 tourist beds in the capital, Nairobi, and around 10 000 on the coast.

In order to promote Kenya's tourist attractions abroad, there are tourist offices in several foreign capitals, including London, Paris and Bonn.

Not surprisingly, most visitors are wealthy tourists from Europe and North America (Fig. 3.52). They visit Kenya in search of their 'idea' of Africa. Foremost in this 'idea' is Africa's wildlife. Together with neighbouring Tanzania and Uganda, Kenya has the richest and largest animal fauna in the world, including the 'big five' – elephant, lion, buffalo, leopard and rhino. In a country which is

Figure 3.52 Origin of tourists to Kenya

Others
Asia
East Africa
North America
Other Africa
UK
Other Europe
West Germany

twice the size of the UK, there is also the attraction of magnificent and varied
scenery. Mount Kenya (Fig. 3.56b) has snowfields and glaciers despite lying astride
the equator, and Kilimanjaro, Africa's highest and most beautiful mountain, is just
across the border in Tanzania. Other attractions include the Great Rift Valley,
forests and grassy plains, moorlands of the high plateaux, and coral beaches along
the coast of the Indian Ocean.

In Kenya 5% of the country is set aside for wildlife conservation, and altogether there are 40 national parks and reserves (including several marine parks),
covering an area larger than Switzerland. The most important conservation areas
are the national parks and national game reserves (Fig. 3.53). The national *parks*
are set aside *exclusively* for wildlife: no cattle or settlements are allowed.
National *reserves* are also protected areas with no hunting, but conservation laws
are less strict, and cattle and settlements are permitted.

Tourism is based on safaris in the interior, and beach holidays along the coast.
A safari holiday involves travelling by mini-bus on dirt tracks through the bush,
and observing and photographing the animals. Safaris are so popular that the
government is becoming concerned about the effects of tourism on the animals,
and the damage to vegetation caused by large numbers of vehicles in some areas.
It is now illegal to drive off the road in bush country in search of wild animals.
Overnight accommodation is in wooden game-lodges which are essentially look-
out posts for animals. Most have a waterhole or river nearby to attract the
animals. The Indian Ocean beaches between Mombasa and Malindi are an
increasingly popular tourist destination, particularly with the development of an
international airport at Mombasa. Temperatures at sea-level are high throughout
the year and modern hotels have been built close to the beaches (Fig. 3.56a) .
Among the attractions are big-game fishing, sub-aqua and surfing.

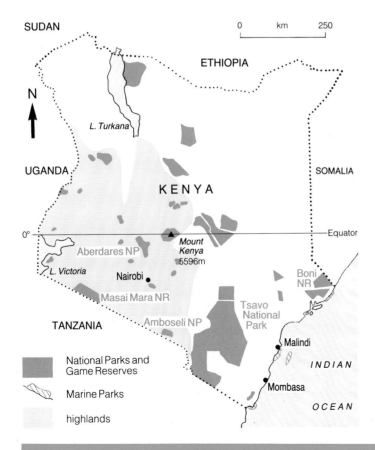

Figure 3.53 Kenya national parks
and national game reserves

Exercise

Study the climate graph of Nairobi (Fig. 3.54).

1 Why are the monthly temperatures at Nairobi a) so constant (clue: look at the latitude of Nairobi in Figure 3.49), b) relatively cool, given its equatorial location.

2 Suggest reasons why April and May are not popular months for safari holidays.

3 January and February are the most popular months for safari. This is a period of drought, when the savanna grasses die back, and water becomes scarce. Can you suggest how this might benefit tourists on safari?

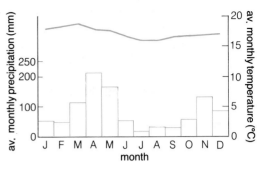

Figure 3.54 Climate of Nairobi (1870 metres)

Tourist issues in Kenya

The issues associated with tourism are both economic and environmental.

Economic

The main economic issue concerns the benefit which Kenya gains from tourism. It can be argued that much of the profit 'leaks' overseas to the rich developed world. For example, lack of money and skills means that foreign airlines fly the tourists to Kenya, foreign tour operators organise package holidays, and special food and clothing for the tourists has to be imported. Altogether, of the £200 million earned by tourism in a year, probably little more than a half remains in Kenya and benefits its people.

Environmental

Conservation of Kenya's wildlife is crucial to the success of tourism. At the moment, there is a serious threat from rapid population growth, which puts great pressure on the land. As more forest is cleared for fuel-wood, and more woodland and grassland are used from cultivation and grazing, habitats for wildlife begin to disappear. Meanwhile overgrazing (for example among the Masai cattle herders) eventually transforms the savanna grasslands into worthless scrub (Fig. 3.56c).

Increasingly, cultivators and livestock herders are encroaching on the savannas, which were formerly left to wildlife. In some cases low world prices for cash crops such as coffee, as well as population pressure, has forced farmers to leave the highlands and grow maize as a food crop in the savanna grasslands. Even worse, from the conservationist's view, the government plans to use one-third of the country for ranching in future. As cattle, sheep and goats compete for grazing with the wild animals, the wildebeest, gazelles and other antelopes will be pushed out. As they disappear, so too will the predators, such as lions and leopards, which depend on them. This is thought to be the main reason for the decline of the leopard and cheetah in Kenya.

Although Kenya has strengthened its laws to protect wildlife – making it illegal, for example, to sell game trophies and ivory, and employing an army of wardens and rangers to combat poaching – the total ban on hunting which exists is actually causing harm to wildlife. The difficulties faced by the Boni people of eastern Kenya highlights this problem. Their traditional way of life has always been one of hunting and gathering, rather than cultivation. However, the ban on hunting has forced them to adopt a slash-and-burn method of cultivation. Not only does this provide a poor living, it also destroys the forests on which the wildlife depend.

Land which has been cleared is so infertile that it can only be cultivated for a year or so, before it has to be abandoned. In this way the Boni destroy up to 80 hectares of forest a year, and the home of countless animals. However, traditional hunters like the Boni, using simple weapons, present no direct threat to wildlife. The real menace is poachers with high-powered rifles, who between 1972 and 1980 in this part of Kenya slaughtered 17 000 elephants, reducing their numbers by nearly 80%.

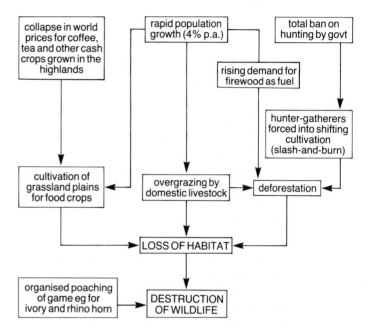

Figure 3.55 Destruction of wildlife and habitats in Kenya

Figure 3.56a Luxury hotel on the Kenyan coast

Figure 3.56b Mount Kenya, Kenya's highest mountain. Although lying astride the equator, Mount Kenya supports a permanent snowfield, with a number of small glaciers.

Figure 3.56c Overgrazed pastures beyond the fence which marks the boundary of the Lake Nakuru national park, Kenya

Figure 3.56d Wildebeeste migration in the Masai Mara National Reserve

Figure 3.56e Black rhino, poached for its horn

Exercise

The solution to the conflict between people and wildlife in Kenya will depend on the *values* held by government decision makers. Three different value positions are listed below:
- The well-being of people should always take priority over that of wildlife.
- Wildlife and its habitats should be protected at all costs.
- Careful planning should promote *both* the welfare of people and the conservation of wildlife.

1 Which of these values do you think lies behind the policies of the Kenyan government?

2 Which of these values is closest to your own? Explain why you hold this particular value (ie say what your beliefs are) and whether you agree or disagree with the policies of the Kenyan government.

3 Examine Figure 3.55 which explains the origins of wildlife and habitat destruction in Kenya. What, in your view, is the root cause of the problem, and what steps should be taken to improve the situation in the long term?

Exercise

Read the article on the poaching of black rhino in Africa.

1 In which country is rhino conservation most likely to succeed? Explain why.

2 What in the writer's view is the cause of rhino poaching?

3 Explain in a short paragraph the attitude of the writer towards the poachers.

Are we going to save the rhino or not?

It is all too easy to confuse symptoms with root causes. The man with the axe, hacking the horns off a dead rhino, is a symptom. So, too, is the corrupt businessman or government official who pays him. And so, too, in a sense, is the high price commanded by rhino horn and other products — up to US$30,000 per kg in its ultimate form in the Far East, or $15,000 for a Yemeni djambia with a rhino-horn handle.

The root of the problem is the imbalance between the more developed world's wealth and Africa's poverty. It is a fair bet that most readers of this feature will perceive the problem of rhino poaching within the context of their own circumstances — will live in a country with a per capita income of at least $10,000 per year.

But if rhino conservation is to succeed, conservationists throughout the developed world *must* acquire a deeper understanding of the milieu within which rhino poaching occurs. Kenya's annual per capita income is $309. Zambia's, $570. And Zimbabwe's — higher than most, and perhaps it is not coincidental that this is where rhino conservation may be most likely to succeed — is $640. And these figures are only as high as they are because of those countries' urban élites. The bulk of their populations are rural, earning maybe $100 a year, if they are lucky. African wildlife does not exist in a fairytale paradise of untouched wilderness. It survives precariously, in island reserves surrounded by seas of poverty.

Figure 3.57 Extract from *BBC Wildlife*, May 1988 (article by Dick Pitman)

Summary

In the more developed countries, the demand for recreation and leisure is rising rapidly. This demand has been fuelled by longer holidays, increased prosperity, and cheaper transport. Such a trend puts pressure on the countryside and coast, which needs to be protected both *for* the enjoyment of visitors, as well as *against* them. In the UK these developments have led to the creation of protected landscapes such as national parks, AONBs and heritage coasts. At a local scale, small country parks have been set aside exclusively for recreation by day-trippers living in nearby towns and cities.

As the cost of air transport has fallen, foreign holidays have become increasingly popular. The tourist attractions of many countries are closely linked to their environmental resources, particularly climate, scenery and wildlife. While the growth of foreign tourism has undoubtedly benefited these countries (including the UK) it has led to the decline of the traditional seaside resort in northern Europe. Elsewhere, rapid and unplanned tourism growth has created problems such as strip development, untidy urban sprawl and damage to the environment.

Many less developed countries have also experienced a tourist boom in recent years. Tourism brings much needed income and employment to these countries and is encouraged by governments who see it as a springboard to economic development. However, the benefits of tourism may be limited. Not only is tourism an uncertain industry, dependent on the prosperity of the more developed countries, but much of the profit flows overseas to foreign hotel owners, suppliers, tour operators and airlines.

Further exercises

A

1 What is a national park?

2 Name two national parks in England south of a line from the Wash to the Mersey.

3 Why was it thought necessary to establish national parks in England and Wales?

B

With reference to the Yorkshire Dales national park:

1 Use diagrams to explain the formation of two landforms which are attractive to visitors.

2 Describe any conflicts of interest which have arisen as a result of the demands for space from different activities.

C

Seasonal unemployment is a problem in many traditional seaside resorts.

1 In which season is unemployment likely to be highest?

2 With reference to a resort you have studied, describe two measures which have been taken to reduce seasonal unemployment.

D

1 What do you understand by the term package holiday?

2 How have package holidays helped the growth of tourism in Spain?

3 The rapid development of tourism in Spain in the 1960s and 1970s brought with it a number of problems.
a Describe these problems.
b Explain how they are being overcome.

E

Compare foreign tourism in Spain and Switzerland using the following headings: number of tourists; tourist attractions; distribution of tourist centres; seasonality.

F

Tourism has become a feature of many less developed countries in recent years. With reference to one example:

1 Describe the main tourist attractions.

2 Explain the growth of tourism.

3 Describe some of the problems tourism has brought.

Checklist of what you should know about recreation and leisure

Key ideas	Examples
The demand for recreation and leisure activities is increasing rapidly in developed countries.	Increasing amounts of free time, higher living standards and cheaper travel are responsible for this change.
Free time comes in blocks: the size of the blocks influences the nature of recreational activities.	Small blocks of free time can only be used for short half-day and day trips. Large blocks can be used for tourist-type recreation and leisure activities, involving overnight stays.
Areas set aside for the conservation of landscapes and wildlife, and for the enjoyment of the public, vary in their scale.	National parks and AONB's in England and Wales. National parks and national reserves in Kenya. Local recreation provision through country parks in England and Wales.
Conservation areas vary in their purposes.	National parks in England and Wales have been created primarily to protect their landscapes, and are often found in remote areas. Country parks have been set up for recreation and the convenience of the public and are located close to large centres of population. Kenyan national parks are designed to protect wildlife and habitats.
Conflict between different land uses in conservation areas leads to controversial issues.	The conflicts between conservation and water supply, recreation, quarrying and farming in national parks and AONBs in England and Wales. In Kenya, the conflict between the conservation of wildlife and the destruction of vegetation by cultivation and overgrazing.
Conflicts can only be resolved through effective planning and management.	The National Park Committees (NPCs) in national parks in England and Wales.
Resources for tourism are both natural and man-made.	Natural resources include climate, beaches, beautiful scenery and wildlife. Man-made resources include historic buildings, museums, leisure parks, local customs and cultures, etc.
Tourism is an international and rapidly growing industry.	There is an increasing proportion of tourists from developed countries who take holidays abroad. Rapid growth of international tourism has been promoted by package deals involving cheap air travel.
Traditional holiday resorts in developed countries are confronted by a number of serious problems.	Decline in the number of domestic tourists. Seasonal unemployment. Pollution of beaches and bathing water.
Traditional holiday resorts are making strenuous efforts to solve these problems.	The development of indoor leisure centres, hobby and activity holidays, and conference facilities. Improved systems of sewage treatment and disposal.
The rapid growth of international tourism in some countries has been unplanned, and has caused problems.	The example of Spain and thoughtless tourism: eg strip development along the coast, high rise hotels, lack of essential services, sprawling villa development.

Key ideas	Examples
Tourism is an important part of the economy of many less developed countries.	Tourism has been encouraged and planned by governments in many less developed countries, including Barbados and Kenya. Tourism provides employment, valuable foreign currency, improved roads and airports, etc.
It is often difficult for less developed countries to ensure maximum benefits for their people from tourism.	The leakage of profits overseas owing to dependence on foreign tour operators and hotel owners, foreign airlines, imported food for tourists, etc.

Subject index

Place index